Also by Jim Crumley

NATURE WRITING
Nature's Architect
The Eagle's Way
The Great Wood
The Last Wolf
The Winter Whale
Brother Nature
Something Out There
A High and Lonely Place
The Company of Swans
Gulfs of Blue Air
The Heart of the Cairngorms
The Heart of Mull
The Heart of Skye
Among Mountains
Among Islands
Badgers on the Highland Edge
Waters of the Wild Swan
The Pentland Hills
Shetland – Land of the Ocean
Glencoe – Monarch of Glens
West Highland Landscape
St Kilda
ENCOUNTERS IN THE WILD SERIES:
Fox / Barn Owl / Swan / Hare

MEMOIR
The Road and the Miles

URBAN LANDSCAPE
Portrait of Edinburgh
The Royal Mile

The
Nature of
Autumn

Jim
Crumley

Saraband

Published by Saraband
Suite 202, 98 Woodlands Road,
Glasgow, G3 6HB, Scotland
www.saraband.net

Editor: Craig Hillsley

ISBN: 9781910192467
ebook: 9781910192474

Printed in the EU on sustainably sourced paper.

1 2 3 4 5 6 7 8 9 10

Contents

Part One

September

Chapter One

A Child of Autumn

I WAS BORN IN MIDSUMMER, but I am a child of autumn. One September day in the fourth or fifth autumn of my life there occurred the event that provided my earliest memory, and – it is not too extravagant a claim – set my life on a path that it follows still. I was standing in the garden of my parents' prefab in what was then the last street in town on the western edge of Dundee. An undulating wave of farmland that sprawled southwards towards Dundee from the Sidlaw Hills was turned aside when it washed up against the far side of the road from the prefab, whence it slithered away south-west on a steepening downhill course until it was finally stopped in its tracks by the two-miles-wide, sun-silvered girth of the Firth of Tay at Invergowrie Bay. Then as now, the bay was an autumn-and-winter roost for migrating pink-footed geese from Iceland; then as now, one of their routes to and from the feeding grounds amid the fields of Angus lay directly over the prefab roof.

I can remember what I was wearing: a grey coat with a dark blue collar and buttons and a dark blue cap. So we were probably going out somewhere.

Why am I so sure it was September and not any other month of autumn or winter or early spring? Because it was the first time, and because for the rest of that autumn and winter and early spring, and ever since, the sound of geese over the house – any house – has sent me running to the window or the garden. So was established my first and most enduring ritual of obeisance in thrall to nature's cause. And so I am as sure as I can be that the very first time was also the first flight of geese over the house after their return from Iceland that September; that September when I looked up at the sound of wild geese overhead and – also for the first time – made sense of the orderly vee-shapes of their flight as they rose above the slope of the fields, the slope of our street, up into the morning sunshine; vee-shapes that evolved subtly into new vee-shapes, wider or longer and narrower, or splintered into smaller vee-shapes or miraculously reassembled their casual choreography into one huge vee-shape the whole width of childhood's sky.

But then there were other voices behind me and I turned towards them to discover that all the way back down the sky towards the river and as far as I could see, there were more and more and more geese, and they kept on coming and coming and coming. The sound of them grew and grew and grew and became tidal, waves of birds like a sea (I knew about the sea by then, for it lived in Arbroath like my Auntie Mary), but a sea where the sky should be, and some geese came so low overhead that their wingbeats were as a rhythmic undertow to their waves of voices, and that too was like the sea.

When they had gone, when the last of them had arrowed away north-east and left the dying embers of the their voices trailing behind them on the air, a wavering diminuendo that fell into an eerie quiet, I felt the first tug of a life-force that I now know to be the pull of the northern places of the earth. And in that silence I stepped beyond the reach of my first few summers and I became a child of autumn.

Now, in the autumn of my life myself, every overhead skein of wild geese – *every* one – harks me back to that old September, and I effortlessly reinhabit the body and mind-set of that moment of childhood wonder. Nothing else, nothing at all, has that effect. I had a blessed childhood, the legacy of which is replete with good memories, but not one of them can still reach so deep within me as the first of all of them, and now, its potency only strengthens.

It would have been about thirty years ago that I first became aware of the Angus poet Violet Jacob, and in par-ticular of her poem, *The Wild Geese*. It acquired a wider audience through the singing of folksinger Jim Reid, who set it to music, retitled it *Norlan' Wind,* and included it on an album called *I Saw the Wild Geese Flee*. I used to do a wee bit of folk singing and I thought that if ever a song was made for someone like me to sing it was that one, but I had trouble with it from the start. My voice would crack by the time I was in the third verse, and the lyrics of the last verse would prick my eyes from the inside. The last time I sang it was the time I couldn't finish it.

Years later, I heard the godfather of Scottish folk sing-ing, Archie Fisher, talking about a song he often sang called *The Wounded Whale*, and how he had to teach himself to sing it "on automatic pilot", otherwise it got the better of him, but I never learned that trick. Even copying out the words now with Violet Jacob's own idiosyncratic spelling, I took a deep breath before the start of the last verse, which is the point where the North Wind turns the tables on the Poet in their two-way conversation:

The Wild Geese

"Oh tell me what was on your road, ye roarin' norlan' Wind,
As ye cam' blawin' frae the land that's niver frae my mind?
My feet they traivel England, but I'm deein' for the north."
"My man, I heard the siller tides rin up the Firth o' Forth."

"Aye, Wind, I ken them weel eneuch, and fine they fa' and
  rise,
And fain I'd feel the creepin' mist on yonder shore that lies,
But tell me, as ye passed them by, what saw ye on the way?"
"My man, I rocked the rovin' gulls that sail abune the Tay."

"But saw ye naethin', leein' Wind, afore ye cam' to Fife?
There's muckle lyin' 'yont the Tay that's dear to me nor life."
"My man, I swept the Angus braes ye hae'na trod for years."
"O Wind, forgi'e a hameless loon that canna see for tears!"

"And far abune the Angus straths, I saw the wild geese flee,
A lang, lang skein o' beatin' wings wi' their heids towards
  the sea,
And aye their cryin' voices trailed ahint them on the air —"
"O Wind, hae maircy, hud yer whisht, for I daurna listen
  mair!"

⊙ ⊙ ⊙

It is the 31st of August, 2015, and the weatherman on the BBC News Channel has just said:

"Tomorrow is the beginning of Meteorological Autumn."

I am unprepared for this news. I have never heard of Meteorological Autumn. I was unaware until this moment that it occurs in the calendar every year, like Lent or National Chip Week. I am wondering whether or not to believe the weatherman. After all, he is often wrong about the weather. I consult the window without moving. There *are* yellow leaves on the one birch tree I can see, and is it my imagination or are there more of them than there were at this time last year? It has been a rubbish summer and maybe that encourages the leaves to do their autumn thing early? Or maybe he's right, and maybe I should begin my autumn tomorrow just as he is obviously beginning his?

A book about autumn has been photosynthesising in my brain for a few years, painstakingly metamorphosing at its own speed, changing shape, changing colour, drinking in moisture from the air around itself, the way it has always seemed to me that a book about autumn should. Why autumn? Because it is my preferred season of the year, my preferred portion of nature's scheme of things, nature's state of grace. Because autumn, in my mind, is a tapped kaleidoscope, a shifting sorcery of shapes and shades, a revitalising of the wild year after the too-long dirge of late summer, a maker of daring moods. Because if a human life can be represented by the poets and the songwriters as a year, and I am in the autumn of that year myself (it is undeniable), then what better time? And because now I have the BBC weatherman poking me in the ribs, and I had better not be late if autumn shows up tomorrow, the first of September, 2015.

Besides, autumn is a magic trick. Science will scoff at such a notion and confront you with the vocabulary of photosynthesis (the synthesis of organic chemical compounds from carbon dioxide using radiant energy, *especially* light; *specifically* the formation of carbohydrates in the chlorophyll-containing tissues of plants exposed to light – or, at least, so says my *Penguin English Dictionary*), which will include super-efficient evaporation, carotenoids, anthocyanins, decomposition of carbohydrates, oxidised tannins, soluble sugars, starches, cellulose, lignum and a complex exchange of gases. But science doesn't know what I know, and what I know is that autumn is a magic trick we call "leaf".

Chapter Two

Autumn Leaves

LEAVES MUST PRODUCE FOOD out of thin air, or else there is
no tree. Luckily for nature and all of us, they are extraordinarily good at it. There is, for example, a stupendously
beautiful oak tree at Ariundle, within the Sunart Oakwoods
of coastal Argyll, that is perhaps eighty feet tall and of a still
mightier girth of limbs. It is also an old acquaintance of
mine. Consider first that the whole edifice is the work of
its leaves, and that no leaf lives longer than six months.
Then marvel at nature. Then believe in magic.

Leaves begin life tight-packed in a bud. In spring, they
start to expand, then they start to draw the sap up through
the tree.

How do they do that?

That is absolutely my favourite tree question. Because
the answer is that no one knows. We can split the atom
and fly to the moon and find water on Mars but we don't
know how a leaf drags a tree up into the air. I find that
profoundly reassuring.

The containing scales of the bud respond to the pressure from within and hinge backwards allowing the leaves
within to open, at which point they go to work, which is
food-shopping. Look again at the eighty-feet-high oak tree

and take a wild guess at how many tons of timber it holds aloft in a crazy fan shape of idolatrous sun-worship. Almost all of it, perhaps as much as ninety-five per cent – the fabulous girth of the trunk and almost every bough, limb, branch, twig and twiglet – is nothing more than carbohydrates ensnared from the air by leaves. Before any one leaf is even half-grown, it has stored up more sustenance than it will need for the rest of its life, but it goes on food-shopping because that is what leaves are born to do, and it donates everything else throughout its life to the tree.

Photosynthesis insists that the action of sunlight on the leaf impregnates its water-filled vessels with chlorophyll (which, incidentally, is why leaves are green), a process that in turn exchanges hydrogen from the water with carbon and oxygen from the air. Photosynthesis needs a certain amount of evaporation to take place, but leaves are so super-efficient at evaporation that they deliver infinitely more than photosynthesis needs. As they lose water to the air they also draw it up through the tree, up through that trunk, through those boughs, limbs, branches, twigs and twiglets; they circulate sap all through the tree, they even draw water through the roots and out of the soil (dissolved soil minerals are the tree's other source of food). Trees consume unimaginable quantities of carbon dioxide. This is why planting unimaginable quantities of trees will save the planet. Carbon is the tree's primary food source, as well as the source of soluble sugars and starches that can be stored or converted to cellulose strengthened with lignin, which makes the thing we call wood, adding a ring to the girth of the trunk every year. This is why we can tell the age of a felled tree.

Then autumn kicks in, and all that stops. It stops because the leaf stops producing chlorophyll, with the immediate result that the green starts to fade. If you make a study of turning leaves on an autumn tree, you will see that the green survives longest in the veins. Green is replaced by a yellow pigment called carotenoid, or a red one called anthocyanin, or both, (and often it is noticeable how the sunniest parts of the tree change colour first and those in deeper shade linger greener for longer). When the yellows and the reds and the indeterminate pinks and oranges have had their fling, decomposed carbohydrates and oxidised tannins turn autumn leaves brown. In a tranquil and all-but-windless early autumn like 2015, huge clusters of leaves turned brown on the tree, and they would come away in your hand in their dozens and flutter uselessly at your feet, their show over, their race run. Or so you might think.

But I am getting ahead of myself. The TV weatherman has told me that tomorrow is the first day of Meteorological Autumn, and I, with a book about autumn to write, don't want to miss it, just in case he's right. So I went out into one of my friendly neighbourhood oakwoods (there are two a few miles apart), and although it was still as green as it was on the last day of summer, there on the ground were my first two brown leaves, except that one still had a single green lobe and the other one was still half yellow. I picked them up and took them home, where I write on an oak table. Both were a lighter shade of brown than the table. It took seven weeks for the yellow half to fade to brown completely, although it is still paler brown than the rest of the leaf, and there is still the faintest green discolouration on the other leaf. Both are beside me as I write and both are now darker than the table. They have curled up at the edges, but rather than become friable, as I had imagined they would, they are waxy and tough. They were joined a couple of weeks later by a tiny vee-shaped twig, two inches long with one green acorn still lodged in its cup and two empty acorn cups; and on the table the acorn soon fell out and also turned brown. And these have become emblematic of the endeavour, emblematic of the magic trick. The acorn is the length of my thumbnail and half as wide, yet it has an eighty-feet oak tree inside it. When this book is written, I will plant it somewhere it can fulfil its potential.

There is a second magic trick to the Ariundle oak. As its leaves thin at the height of autumn and dance to boisterous, salty onshore winds, the inner tracery of branches and twigs hidden away since early spring begins to reappear, and the sky beyond the tree begins to re-emerge as fragments wedged between the branches and twigs, as thousands of shards a dozen shades of blue, grey, white, sunrise red and sunset purple. Here, in such a tree was surely the genesis of stained glass, and the teeming tracery, black against the sky, became the black lead of stained glass windows. The oak tree in question stands on a hillside so that you can look up into it from below the level of its roots, a viewpoint from which the analogy of great cathedral east windows is irresistible.

The forest is like a cathedral. How often have nature poets reached for that too-ready metaphor, too-ready and wrong? Wrong because the reality is the other way round

– the cathedral nave is like the forest. How long ago did a stonemason with a visionary cast to his trade walk home with his tools on his shoulder through a grove of tall, straight trunks, and, looking up, see in his mind's eye not trees but columns of stone?

And how long thereafter did he, or another in another town or another land, stop before an oak tree like this giant of Ariundle with late autumn tints among the thinning leaves, a thousand patches of sky ensnared among the branches, and shafts of sunlight prodding apart the canopy, so that he fell to his knees and dared to give voice to his vision: "Stained glass!"

It was an idea that would travel the world. Chartres, Cologne, Kirkwall, Washington, Amsterdam, Salisbury, Edinburgh, Durham, York. And in 1960s Coventry the whole idea was spectacularly reinvented by Basil Spence and Graham Sutherland as tapestry.

With all this swilling in the nature writer's mind as I wrote it down at my oak table with the leaves and acorn and the three empty acorn cups, the miracle – the magic – of the whole improbably, blindingly astounding process lit up the whole room. "I believe in God but I spell it Nature," said Frank Lloyd Wright. So do I. So did the stonemason who turned trees into columns of stone, so did the stained glass artist. The cathedral is like the autumn forest.

◎ ◎ ◎

The first day of autumn exhales with a berry-breath and all nature catches the scent. It is always the air that announces the change. It sharpens, cools and gently startles. It smells of hedgehogs. The light yellows, a pale yellow that will deepen as the season settles into its stride. Yesterday was not like this. Yesterday was the last rites of summer – old, done, defeated, frayed-at-the-edges, sleepwalking-towards-the-abyss, hollow-in-the-middle, holed below the waterline summer. Good riddance.

And the first day of autumn is the beginning of everything, the first stirrings of rebirth. The forest fall (it is better named in America than here) thickens the land with limitless tons of bits and pieces of trees. The earth is hungry for these, for they break down into food: all spring, all summer, it has been thrusting life upwards and outwards, and by the last day of summer, it is tired. Autumn is the earth's reviver and replenisher, the first day of autumn is the new beginning of everything and the last day of autumn is the beginning of next spring. Autumn is the indispensable fulcrum of nature's year.

So I was summoned by the oakwoods, for oakwoods are the first theatre of autumn. The oaks at Woodland Trust Scotland's Glen Finglas reserve in the Trossachs are steeply clustered along the lower slopes of hills that reach 2,000 feet. It was there that I chose to go to test the weatherman's theory, my first destination on what would become a long and more or less non-stop journey through autumn.

Infant trees were all around me, their gestures anything but grand: ankle-high rowans (new-minted greens and cracked rust and every photosynthetic shade in between – autumn is a madcap, haphazard season in the undergrowth), knee-high hollies (friend of wren and ladybird) rooted in fat, lime-green blancmanges of moss that clustered around shady oak roots, birch saplings (thousands and thousands of these – a birchwood is nature's default position hereabouts) whose crowns narrowed the path and rubbed my shoulders and whose leaves were as golden as they were green. In the midst of so much burgeoning infant life, an eight-feet-high, limbless, headless and all-but-dead-on-its-feet sycamore torso still stood, still summoned the paltry life force that thrusts spindly twigs directly sideways without the intervention of branches; these twitched right in front of my eyes in a hidden and shadowed bend in the path and they wore a thin coat of leaves – washed-out and yellow, and freckled with black and brown, and fragile, the last gesture of a last gesture. The wind shivered among them for a moment and they danced fitfully to its soft, sad song. However long autumn allowed them (and it would not be many days now), theirs had been a dance in a beautiful coat.

A tree fifty yards ahead, and partially obscured by a dozen others and their networks and clusters of branches and leaves, just moved in an eye-catching, instinct-rousing way. Eye and instinct fused to form my one indispensable life-support system, my all-season-all-weather shadow. I never go out without it and it is forever muttering in my ear. What it had just told me was that the movement in question was not the tree itself, but rather something *of* the tree. It had come to rest and it was hidden, and it would have to move again – or I would – to reveal its meaning. But stillness is the most useful tool of my trade, and I knew that whatever just moved was on the move in a way that I was not, so I told myself, "It *will* move first" and that in moving it would justify my strategy and answer – or fail to answer – the unarticulated question in my head.

Wait.

Watch.

Listen.

Learn.

⊙ ⊙ ⊙

I had seen nothing arrive, nothing that flew in or ran up the trunk, but that does not mean that nothing flew in or that nothing ran up the trunk, it just means that I didn't see it arrive. And there is always the possibility, of course, that it was there all the time and there had been no arrival for me to see. But it was there now, however it may have arrived, and its movement had an effect on the tree and *that* was what caught my eye and roused my instinct.

A stand-off like this, if it is not resolved quickly, creates a kind of tension that stems from simultaneously knowing and not knowing. I know that something moved and that oak leaves rippled outwards and downwards in response. I do not know what moved and I do not know if whatever-it-was knows I am here and, if so, whether it is troubled by my presence. Instinct says no, it does not know and is not troubled, and therefore its subsequent stillness is relaxed, rather than a stillness that is terrified to move.

And then it moved.

And then it laughed.

It appeared from behind the tree's trunk no more than a yard off the ground and in that tree's shade, but almost at once it burst into sunlight. Precisely at that moment something odd occurred, time stalled, and I began to see it with a quite startling clarity and apparently in slow motion. It was as if the perceptive resources of all my senses were simultaneously heightened and I had acquired the power to control the pace of events as they unfolded. I cannot explain the circumstances any better than that, although, occasionally, I have been the subject of such a visitation before, or at least of something similar. Each time I have been alone, each time I have been prompted by instinct into an awareness of something about to happen, and each time (I have used the analogy before and have found no better way of expressing it) I have felt as if nature was tapping me on the shoulder with an implicit instruction: "Watch this."

So I had stilled myself in response to the rippling oak leaves and waited, and waited, and then it moved and then laughed and then it appeared much lower than I had expected, and then it flew from shadow into sunlight, and then it inexplicably slowed down. In this new state of heightened awareness I saw its head crane sideways with a twist of its neck and almost at right angles so that it looked directly down the line of the path in my direction. I saw one wing-tip dip, the other rise then the whole sun-glittered body of the creature fell into line-astern behind the new course of the head and neck and every vivid and clearly defined colour swayed into place – raven black, maple-leaf scarlet, snow-bunting white, larch green, aspen yellow, oak-bark brown. The green woodpecker is a living emblem of early autumn, a fusion of all the shades of photosynthesis with added black and white details, a pop-art, yah-boo, guffawing mocker of the oakwood canopy and the airspaces between the trees.

It began to fly down the path towards me and no more than a yard above the ground, but because I was downhill a bit, it flew exactly at my eye level, even as the path fell away below it. It also flew with that jaunty, bouncing gait of all the woodpecker tribe, from the sparrow-sized lesser-spotted to the crow-sized black woodpecker of Norwegian pinewoods, and I became conscious of my own head nodding in time to the rhythmic fluctuations of altitude and attitude as it rose and fell a few inches with every flap and glide. The overall effect was one of level flight but, in truth, not a single yard of it was level.

At that stage in its flight, there was nothing to indicate that the woodpecker had distinguished my tree-coloured shape from among the many trees massed at my back and to my left and right. Then the head craned left again, that same twist of the neck, the same realignment of body to neck as the bird turned again at right angles, a sudden down-thrust of wings and the bird tilted abruptly backwards and in an attitude more vertical than horizontal, rose into tree shadows again, wings working like a giant, ungainly hummingbird. It perched vertically against the trunk of a rowan well laden with berries. I might have assumed that this was simply a speculative kind of perch from which to re-evaluate the day and the wood and the possibilities of the next meal, which in the green woodpecker's world usually means ants. I *might* have made that assumption were it not for the fact that suddenly I was aware of recent history repeating itself, because ten months before and no more than a quarter of a mile away, something happened that introduced me to this jazzy bird's taste for improvisation.

⊙ ⊙ ⊙

That old November day from last autumn had been playing at volcanoes up on the mountain, lathering its flanks with mist that lolled and rolled and tumbled unpredictably at the whim of a lazy wind. The sun was lazier still, and by mid-afternoon the day was going headlong downhill and sunless and ever deeper into the greyest grasp of deepest November. Meanwhile, as befits volcanic inconvenience, all air traffic was grounded. I had seen one robin in a bramble bush and a hunched pair of bullfinches with their backs to me, which is not a lot to show for two hours of walking in country this wild.

So I crossed the glen's lower-lying and more open side, climbed a short slope through oak trees cluttered with clusters of old foliage the colour of cold tea, much of which will cling on right through the winter. (Why do oaks do that? And why do only some of them do that?) The mist was thinner beyond the trees from where, on any day when views are possible, there is a wide prospect of Trossachs hills. Holes appeared in this thinning veil, through which I could see back across the glen to the mountain mist, so the view was of thin mist and thick mist.

Near the edge of the wood – and this is the point of this historical diversion – there is a fine rowan just where the trees give way to open ground of undulating rough pasture, so I stopped to look at it as I have done many,

many times. Something of the day's lethargy had infiltrated my bones and spirit by this time, so I sat on a rock and decided to drink coffee while I looked at the rowan, and then I would go back. The rowan held a few old leaves, pale-yellowy-gold-mottled-with-brown by now, and also a surprising amount of berries, although these were dark and far past what a rowan-jelly-maker might call their best. But without them, what happened next simply would not have happened.

I scoured the tree and what little I could see of the open ground beyond with the binoculars, searching for something to focus on, some vagrant scrap of life to thwart the evil twins of cold and lethargy, which had taken the day by the throat. I was reconciling myself to the essential truth of an old John Denver lyric that had just insinuated itself into the forefront of my mind from its resting place in one of the stoorier nooks where I let such things lie: something about how some days are diamonds and there are others that are just stones. The relentless, lifeless greyness of the day had "stone" written all over it.

But then I became aware in a vague sort of way that something seemed to have changed out on the grass a dozen yards or so beyond the rowan. Something small and low-down and, as yet, shapeless, and not obviously different in texture and tone from the rough pasture hillside, except that it seemed to be moving, furtively and head-down (much of the movement of the whatever-it-was was obscured by grass in clumps and tussocks and humps; I was rather assuming at this point that the thing would have a head). Then all discernible movement ceased, and I

suspected a trick of the half-light. Then something galvanised, there was a flash of fire that seared through the lowest
airspace just above the grass, then came straight towards
me at eye level, then veered abruptly upwards and left into
the rowan tree, where it perched vertically and metamor-
phosed into a green woodpecker.

"Flash of fire" is a better description by far than "green
woodpecker", and I wish I could claim that I and I alone
had invented it. In fact, all I have done is to translate it
– from Gaelic. *Lasair-choille* is the Gaelic name. *Coille* is
simply a wood. *Lasair* is fire, flame, flash; in any combination that fits the context. In the context of that moment on
that stone-grey hillside, a "flash of fire" was exactly what
had just illuminated my stone-grey day. Besides, as I now
know, if your green woodpecker arrows up from obscurity
on the ground and comes at you at eye level, it is not a
green bird at all that you see but a red and white one – red
skull cap (and cheeks in the male) and white chest. In much
the same way a head-on kingfisher is a brown bird, and
only the water beneath it and the way it is flying suggests
that it might be what it obviously is if you see it from any
other angle at all. And if there was any justice in the nomen-
clature of the world's birds at all, the green woodpecker
would have a kingfisher-ish name, something worthier of
its fire-flashing potential.

Meanwhile, up in the rowan tree, something stirred.
Almost every bird book you ever saw will inform you with
absolute certainty that all green woodpeckers eat is ants,
that ants control every facet of their wellbeing or otherwise, especially ants like the ones that throng the top few

inches of the earth beneath the grass of old, unimproved pasture, like that one beyond the rowan tree. If the ants prosper, so do the green woodpeckers. A dearth of ants is likewise a dearth of green woodpeckers. It's one of nature's fundamental principles; the wellbeing of predators is determined by the wellbeing of prey species. Bird books will also tell you that the green woodpecker is purpose-built to eat nothing but ants: a stabbing beak to open the earth in cone-shaped grooves; and a secret weapon, a cunningly stowed-away, four-inches-long tongue designed to unearth the ants in improbable numbers. The same technique also works in rotten trees where the woodpecker's huge feet allow it to perch vertically, and again, ants are the essential quarry. If the bird book happens to specialise in Scottish birds, it may add that the green woodpecker is open to occasional forays into the Speyside pinewoods, where catching ants around the waist-high anthills is its equivalent of shooting fish in a barrel. The book may not use those words, but that will be the gist. I have yet to see a field guide acknowledge the possibility of a non-ant diet. Yet this one at the far end of my binoculars was eating rowan berries. It also proved remarkably adept at the berry-picking, which suggested to me that it had done it before. Even out-on-a-limb, even out on the outermost edges of out-on-a-limb, the woodpecker negotiated the slenderest of twigs in a slow, sideways glissade to reach the berries at the end, perfectly poised, sure of itself and its technique, and clearly relishing the non-ants that clustered there, the fruits of its labours.

So as I watched I thought about this, about the why and the wherefore, and it took about half a minute of thinking to come to the following conclusion. The green wood-pecker is accustomed to ground-feeding – for ants – but in the course of ground-feeding for ants all it has to do is to stray somewhere near a rowan tree in summer or autumn to find windblown bunches of downcast, eye-catching rowan berries in its path. One speculative stab of that expert beak yields the delightful taste of rowan berries, so it eats all the berries on the ground. It then turns its head sideways to look up (it is a great sideways-and-upwards turner of its head, and this, remember, is a bird that nests in trees, and there-fore understands perfectly that berries and nuts and leaves lying on the ground mostly come from above, from trees). And there was the rowan tree, one grey, misted November day when the ants were few and far between, and there were enough berries to keep body and soul together, and it stands to reason that if the bird scavenged that fretwork of branches often enough, it would get very adept at it.

It is equally possible, I suppose, that the green wood-pecker has watched its spotted cousins gather autumn stashes of pine cones by carrying them individually to an "anvil" rock where it thrashes them open, plucks the seeds and chucks away the cones. This the spotted woodpeckers do in the lean months when the oak trees are not as replete with ants as they are in the spring and summer. Might not the greens resort to the same food source for the same reason? I don't know because I have never seen it, and if the compilers of my bird books know, they're not saying.

But here's a thing: the Gaels distinguish between green and spotted woodpeckers not by their utterly different colour schemes but by their characteristic behaviour, the flash of flame for the green, but the great spotted woodpecker is *snagan-daraich*, the knocker on wood, and specifically on oak. They were good, were they not, the old Gaels, when it came to naming the creatures that shared their world? My favourite is the jay – *sgreuchag-choille*, the screamer of the woods, and I know from the luminous writing of my friend Jim Perrin that it has its mirror image in Welsh – *sgrech coed*. In that spirit the Gaels might just have come up with something like the giggler of the woods in honour of the green woodpecker, for its far-carrying, manic guffaw that sounds as if it might have escaped from a 1950s recording of *The Goon Show*. But luckily for me, the bird-namers came up with *lasair-choille,* and the flash of flame that briefly turned my day of stones into a day of diamonds.

◉ ◉ ◉

So that was the history lesson I brought to bear on the green woodpecker as it angled up from the woodland path to a vertical clasp on the trunk of a shadowed rowan, where its cramponed feet bit into the bark and its rigid tail angled in to the trunk too, so that the stance was well belayed. Then nothing at all happened. The moment bound bird and me together in our two stillnesses about twenty yards apart. The bird's stillness amid tree shadows was ill-suited to that heightened, mercurially slow-motion vision I had somehow contrived out of that brief flight from shadow into sunlight and back into shadow by way of two right-angled turns. Then my own stillness began to feel awkward itself, and that was more troubling. So often in my nature-writing years, a gift for stillness has been my saving grace and it had just handed me that small insight into the nuances of woodpecker flight, but without moving at all I felt the mood splinter and the woodland resumed its natural way of moving in normal time. I am aware that sometimes I try and immerse too deeply into nature's scheme of things and come up short. There are moments, especially in familiar landscapes, when I can see with the clarity of mountain spring water, moments of rarefied access to nature at work. It is tempting to contrive imaginary constructs to explain it away, but the only explanation I believe in is that because I have watched so much for so long, once in a while the quality of the watching rises above the norm on a buoyancy of accumulated experiences, and briefly achieves a kind of perfection. And because it is inevitably a momentary phenomenon, what follows immediately afterwards is – also inevitably – something of a letdown.

And yet almost nothing had changed. The light – the sacred light that graces autumn from its first stirring until prime October – had not changed from those few seconds when it chanced on the luminosity and the palette of the flier. No cloud troubled the sky, no alarm troubled the denizens of the woodland, no breeze nudged the oaks into silence-scarring whispers. But the flight's denouement was in shadows and that ended the privilege of the encounter, and I noticed at once that when the woodpecker's landing induced two slender rowan branches to quiver so that they discarded a dozen pale yellow ready-to-go leaves, these fell at the regular free-fall speed of all downcast autumn leaves.

Chapter Three

The Far East

DRIVING ACROSS THE TAY ROAD BRIDGE from Dundee, the low green hull of Fife's north-facing hills was noticeably patched with the tawny and faded yellow shades of standing crops and cut crops, and with newly ploughed fields the red-brown shades of fox. In other words, the entire palette of oakwood photosynthesis had been laid out like a colour chart on the face of the land itself – chlorophyll to carotenoid to anthocyanin and all their intermediate shades.

Like an Australian Aborigine tracing songlines across the ancestral homelands in search of the Dreamtime, I am helplessly addicted to a migratory route to Scotland's Far East, which threads the low-slung contours of east Perthshire or north Fife along the Firth of Tay to Dundee, and to a frontier of North Sea coast, from Auchmithie in the north to St Monans in the south, that resounds to the three-syllable poetry of kittiwakes and the baying of seals.

Of all the landscapes of my life, this is their common ancestor. Dundee is where I was born and grew up and for all that I have written about Scotland's Highlands and Islands (and I love them dearly), at rock bottom I am an east coast mainlander by birth and inclination and I belong to that cast of Scots who think the sun should rise over the sea, not set in it. I grew tall craning to see mountains in the north and the north-west, and it has long been a source of comfort to me that from the summit of Dundee's centrepiece hill (variously known as Dundee Law, the tautologous but widespread Law Hill, or the local vernacular's preference for The Lah), on the right kind of day, I can see Schiehallion, even as I inhale the salt-laden air on a wind off the sea.

The Tay would lure me west in time and my writing life eventually settled on a tract of Perthshire and Stirlingshire between the upper reaches of Tay and Forth. But all my life I have hankered after the sea, and from the mid-point of the country I have worn a groove from coast to coast between Dundee and Mull with such instinctive longing that surely I am a slave to some age-old, tribal, songline-like ritual. I have heard that, historically, the name Crum was a sept of the MacDonalds of Benderloch, which is Argyll coast opposite Mull, and I have traced my own branch of the Crumleys back to Donegal in the 1790s, whence a couple of them made their way to Dundee around 1840. In the Dundee enclave of Lochee they dug in for the next 120 years. Throughout the centuries-long sea-going heyday of Scotland's West Highland seaboard, Benderloch to Donegal was no distance at all, and the Benderloch MacDonalds thing is perfectly plausible. A consequence of all that is that whenever I weigh anchor and sally forth from the edge-of-the-Highlands heartland, and if my destination is one coast or the other, something of the air of pilgrimage attends the journey, although the nature of the pilgrimage varies radically depending on its direction.

A few days after the green woodpecker in Glen Finglas, and with the glowing gouache of its finery still undimmed in my mind, I travelled east along the north bank of the Tay in the lee of Errol's waving walls of reed beds, dawdling in their shadow because the road was narrow and empty and the whole day was at my command, and the wind in the reeds was a soft roar at my elbow as it leaned on the open car window. I drove into the emblematic sea-born sunrise that burnished the widening sea-going miles of the Tay beyond the reeds, and these were back-lit and topped with shades of flame. At that point, the river is a boulevard between reed-smothered banks, for these are the largest reed beds anywhere in Britain, and a very specialised micro-habitat all of their own with a unique wildlife community. Hefty, agile, vee-winged marsh harriers and furtive packs of bearded tits are the star attractions through spring and summer, but it is the reed beds themselves, their sheer quantity and extent and stature, that turn heads. They planted a momentary image in my mind of something exotically Middle Eastern that had me rummaging among half-remembered imagery from Gavin Maxwell's masterpiece wrought from the waterworld of Iraq's Marsh Arabs, *A Reed Shaken by the Wind* (Longmans, 1957; Eland Publishing Ltd, 2003) Later that day, back among my own bookshelves, I would correct my careless remembrance with the real thing in my hands:

...we were moving through open blue lagoons fringed and islanded with giant golden reeds growing dense and twenty feet high. They were as ripe standing corn must appear to a

mouse, huge and golden in the sun, with only a tiny fringe of
new green growth in the blue water at their feet…the confin-
ing reed beds at the farther side looked like long yellow cliffs
of sand…

I had a short meeting in Crail on the Fife coast that day, but either side of it the day was given over to a leisurely exploration of the first stirrings of a Lowland autumn. So I had edged slowly between the river and the flat fields of the Carse of Gowrie that sprawled away northwards to the feet of the first of all my hills, my forever-friends, the Sidlaws. At Dundee, I turned south across the Tay Road Bridge, and there was autumn at its far end. I turned east again to follow the river towards the coast. Estuary becomes open sea at Tentsmuir, a pinewood that wades into a fringe of sand dunes. These, in turn, relent into a vast sandy beach. Its outermost reaches are huge sandbanks internationally renowned as breeding grounds for both grey and common seals. The autumn seascape – and the waters of the estuary – had just begun to adjust to the arrival of vast numbers of waders and wildfowl, including densely packed rafts of eider ducks thousands strong. By midwinter, anything up to 20,000 will have gathered, an unforgettable and indelible presence. You never quite know what to expect when you step from the trees onto the dunes and thread a way through them and finally step out onto the open beach to confront the triple expanses of sand and open sea and open sky, arranged in immense horizontals: the tricolour of nature's national flag. I imagine someone like Mark Rothko confronting it for the first time and thinking to himself:

"No, I need bigger canvasses. Much, much bigger canvasses." And when he got them he filled them with immense horizontals. As far as I know, he was never here, but he was one of the New York School so he had the western Atlantic seaboard at his disposal, so who knows? Besides, he was famously reluctant to explain the motivation behind his huge abstracts. A recent retrospective of his work at the National Gallery of Art in Washington offered this perspective, which corresponds (albeit in slightly more academic terms than I could muster) with what happens to me when I step out onto Tentsmuir beach:

> *Alternately radiant and dark, Rothko's art is distinguished by a rare degree of sustained concentration on pure pictorial properties such as colour, surface, proportion, and scale, accompanied by the conviction that those elements could disclose the presence of a high philosophical truth. Visual elements such as luminosity, darkness, broad space, and the contrast of colours, have been linked...to profound themes such as tragedy, ecstasy, and the sublime...*

I stepped from dunes onto beach and raw space came at me in waves, an almost physical force whose ingredients were as Rothko intended, "colour, surface, proportion, and scale". It is not just the sunrise that distinguishes east coast beaches from those on the west coast, there is also the conspicuous absence of islands. The sense of proportion and scale is overwhelmingly intensified by the absence of a focal point. The pale tawny sand runs away from you across immense distance to south and north. At low tide the sea is far, far out and barely audible. The sand darkens by degrees as it marches eastward towards the rippling line of surf. The sea in the morning is pale and electrified by sunlight. There is almost too much light. I decided to walk out to the edge of the sea and head north to look for seals, knowing that if I did that, and whether I saw seals or not, all kinds of other things would cross my path. I knew that, because they always do.

The approach to the forest from the landward side had felt benevolent and warm, still suffused with souvenirs of old summer. Out on the edge of the land there was a surprising wind blowing up and a surprisingly big sea running, an energising intoxication. It occurs to me again and again as I travel the length and breadth of my own country how eagerly I respond to edges – island shores, the edge of the Highlands, the edge of the land – a sense I first became aware of right here. This is my source country, and so much of this nature-writing life, which has taken me to Alaska and back, has its identifiable origins within the force field of the Tay estuary. The debt I owe to my upbringing and its landscape is eternal and unrepayable.

I found seals much sooner than I had expected. Or, rather, I found one seal.

There was a single grey seal bull out on the water, his blunt head and his ruff of chins a kind of marker buoy, indicating the hazard to shipping posed by the better part of 1,000 pounds of flesh and blubber and muscle slung beneath him, beneath the waves, a living iceberg of trouble. He stared directly at me across fifty yards of wave-tops, his eyes a mask behind which he concealed one of the more bizarre relationships with which we bespatter our dealings with nature. Celtic and Norse storytelling is awash with selkies and sirens who cast their sealskins to come ashore as beautiful women and fall for a young man who steals her sealskin, locks it away somewhere safe and traps her ashore, marries her, and they live happily enough until the day she finds the hidden sealskin and returns with it to the sea, leaving bereft husband and children behind; or else they pose on rocks as women and so enrapture helpless sailors that they are lured to their doom.

But the biological reality is *that* out there, that preposterous hunk of seal meat afloat off the Tentsmuir coast, that is what really lights the fire of a grey seal cow, and autumn is their spectacular – and often vicious – mating season. The apparently benign bull, scratching all his chins at once as he gives me his most appraising stare, will become, literally, monstrous in defence of his chosen battlefield and his chosen harem. A fight between two half-crazy bulls turns the surf red with shed blood; their bellowing voices laced with equal parts of fury and pain can momentarily drown out the sound of the surf itself. The victor and vanquished blunder ashore to try and impress the cows, and to lick their many wounds. It is all a ferocious output of energy, so recklessly discharged that newly born pups are often crushed to death in the chaos.

Nothing much of grey seal mating makes much sense to human eyes, and perhaps that in itself explains why, hundreds of years ago, we felt the need to reconcile our response to the admittedly alluring song of the grey seal by concocting the selkie-siren mythology. As recently as the

1990s, my very favourite writer, George Mackay Brown, was still working magical new variations on the ancient theme into his stories and poetry.

A particularly rare characteristic of Tentsmuir is that it accommodates both grey and common seals. The vast area of sand on the beach and sandbanks offers almost limitless scope, and the very different breeding patterns of the two species help to minimise conflict; not that it doesn't happen – it does – but the Tentsmuir situation works better than you might think, and it confounds the theories of many a guidebook writer. So growing up in nearby Dundee offered, among many other things, an early-years education of the whys and wherefores of the seal tribes. It was a long, long time after those early nature study lessons in primary school, or leaning over the railings of the "Fifies" (the long-extinct Tay ferries that plied between Dundee and Newport) to watch the seals basking on the banks or flirting with the bow wave, that I would learn just how much seal blood my home city had on its hands. People have killed seals forever and wherever in the world they have coincided. But the scale of the killing inflicted by 19th-century whaling fleets, including Dundee's, makes grim reading in the 21st century. Dundee eventually accommodated the biggest whaling fleet in Britain, but it was the whaling ships' secondary target of seals that helped the whaling companies to make ends meet. In one year alone – 1881 – the fifteen ships of the Dundee whaling fleet killed more than 150,000 seals on the whaling grounds of Greenland and Newfoundland. The total number throughout the whaling years was well into millions.

Times and attitudes change. By the time Frank Fraser Darling was researching the grey seal colonies on North Rona and the Treshnish Isles just before World War II, the tone of his writings was markedly different from much that had gone before.

"We had come to watch seals and were full of eagerness and joy when the great beasts began to collect about the place in increasing numbers," he wrote in *Island Years* (G. Bell & Sons, 1940; Little Toller, 2011). He wrote with undisguised affection for one colossal bull he called Old Tawny:

> *His personality soon became evident to us…what a magnificent head and proud bearing he had! Never since, either on the Treshnish or on North Rona, have I seen a bull seal to equal him in size or majesty.*
>
> *His movements ashore were delightful to watch – the way he would make himself comfortable on the rock and then the expressive movements of his forelimbs…you would see Old Tawny scratch his belly delicately with his fingernails, waft a fly from his nose, and then, half closing his hand, draw it down over his face and nose just as men often do. Then he would smooth his whiskers with the back of his hand, this side and that…You might see him scratch one palm with the fingers of the other hand, or close his fist and scratch the back of it. A seal's movements are often a most laughable travesty of humanity, but considered more carefully as seal movements, they have great beauty.*

The science of conservation has also taken up the seals' cause, and seal culls amid Scottish waters are mostly a thing of the past. And the educational aspect of National Nature Reserves preaches considerate behaviour towards the seals at Tentsmuir, signs that further symbolise the evolution of our attitudes towards nature. If you are a nature writer born and brought up in a city that once flourished its whaling credentials all over the northern hemisphere, it's not before time.

⊙ ⊙ ⊙

The bull seal slid beneath the surface, and when I saw him again he was a hundred yards further out and easing north towards the seal sandbanks. The long beach and the nearest wave-tops were suddenly thronged with wader birds, and scanning the sea itself with binoculars revealed the autumn's first seriously large raft of eiders. The birds rose and fell through the crests and troughs of the waves, but every rising wave seemed to reveal more and more birds. Counting seabirds is the stuff of ornithological nightmares and I don't even try. But this kind of sudden appearance at the edge of the sea and the edge of the land is characteristic of the restlessness that besets much of the natural world as autumn's summons demands drastic changes of the established order of spring and summer. That awareness, and the unrelenting rituals and sounds of sea and sea winds (these were now making themselves heard among the pines), contributed to the sense of an un-still landscape, a place possessed by an organic restlessness as old as the Earth. Beneath that colossally arched tract of sky (and east coast skies are bigger than anywhere else's this side of Orkney), sea, sand and trees are forever realigning themselves, pushing against each other, testing each other out, reshaping themselves and each other. The effect of all that is of a landscape frontier constantly on the move, both unsettled and unsettling. I turned north and went to look for seals.

I found them out on the furthermost reaches of the fluctuating banks beyond Tentsmuir Point, several hundred greys but not a single common seal in sight. A lingering scrutiny with good binoculars offered an object lesson in colour-coding those seals biologists call "grey", for these ran through the spectrum from almost white to almost orange to as-near-to-black-as-makes-no-difference. There were only a handful of seals in the water. The mass of animals was at rest yet it was also restless. Heads rose and fell and turned to observe every compass point, jaws snapped at other seals and at nothing at all, flippers scratched and groomed, tails wafted or just arched up into the air and paused there with no obvious purpose or means of support. The individuals within the herd constantly changed place or readjusted the space around them, often with bickering, sometimes with biting, yet the collective will of the herd insisted on cramming as many seals as possible into as small a space as possible, safety in densely-packed numbers.

The big black-backed gulls were intrigued by the mass, although it was not clear to me why. They drifted against the wind, slowing almost to stalling speed within inches of the seals' upturned heads. The seals responded with upward lunges and snapping jaws, and the gulls responded in turn by rising a foot out of reach, then dropping again. I wondered if this was a game, a ritual enjoyed by both parties, but it still looked to my admittedly inexpert eyes as if the gulls infuriated the seals for the hell of it and without the possibility of profiting by it.

For the two hours I sat there the gulls maintained their tormenting presence the whole time, while dozens of turnstones ran in among the seals, apparently trying to find food on the seals' bodies. Fraser Darling had spotted the same thing more than sixty years ago, writing in *Island Years*:

Turnstones...remained in my memory as the little companions of the great seals. You would see a seal snap at a gull which might come near it, but the busy little turnstones ran among the seals lying on the rocks or high on the island, pecking morsels from the bodies of the great beasts themselves...

It was good to have Fraser Darling's confirmation of something I had just noticed for the first time, but there was no explanation from him, and there is none from me, about why turnstones alone, of all the wader tribes that throng seal coasts like this one, have identified a seal colony as a source of food, and are tolerated by the seals at such intimately close quarters.

⊙ ⊙ ⊙

Fifty miles to the south-east, on a hidden cliff-girt, boulder-strewn Berwickshire beach one late-November a couple of autumns ago, a sodden gale was flaying the land with sheets of rain, a huge sea was running, and the noise where it head-butted that broken shore was fearful to human ears, fearsome to human eyes. I looked at it from halfway down the cliff. I thought:

"I wouldn't last half a minute in there. They would find me in small pieces strewn everywhere up the coast between here and Tentsmuir."

Yet it was precisely there in the fearful, fearsome midst of that headlong sea's landfall that the grey seals played.

Played?

Yes, I think so. They hauled themselves over rocks so shattered, angular and chaotically stacked that I would have had trouble simply standing up there, but they turned in their own length and heaved into the sea where they were at once fluent and wonderfully agile. They stayed among the breakers and they stayed on the surface, which is not the way of a hunting seal, and they relished the shattering of huge waves, and apparently relished the roar in their ears. In the rarefied world of the grey seals, this is what passes for a nursery. This is where the females gave birth and suckled and taught their young to swim. Everywhere among the rocks there were pups. Most were alone, a few suckled, a handful seemed impossibly far-flung from the centre of that broken bay where the adults congregated. Some looked impossibly trapped, and the next I checked on them they would be a dozen yards away or back in the water.

I was looking for a secure foothold among the highest rocks, a secluded refuge to settle in and watch the nursery at work, when I almost stood on a pup that was further out and higher up the beach than any I had seen. Its immediate response to my sudden arrival was to slide down the rock where it had been reclining, to push itself deeper into a natural cavity among the rocks. Then it turned its back so that instead of its white face I was presented with the grey shades of its back and the back of its head and neck, and at once, it was not a seal but another rock on a beach of rocks. I found a different place to settle and watch.

Several bulls waited for the females just offshore, for mating had begun within a few weeks of the pups being born. As they waited they sparred, and sometimes they sparred so vigorously that they fought, and when they fought the sea reddened around them. The females too were not slow to draw blood if a bull was too enthusiastic before she was ready to receive his enthusiasm. It is difficult to imagine a more untranquil theatre of nature than a grey seal nursery on such a shore and with such a sea running.

The pups grow strong and learn quickly (the ones that are not crushed to death by the mad heavyweight dance of the mating cows and bulls), for not to grow strong and not to learn is to die young. They are improbably young when they abandon the nursery and the adults leave them to their own devices, and they travel improbable distances. Some of these very pups will have travelled to Norway by next spring. You look at them, apparently helpless, you look at the brutal sea that awaits them, and you ask yourself two questions:

How?

Why?

The answers, of course, are known to every grey seal that ever spilled from its mother's milk into such a shore and with such a sea running. It is that secret knowledge, perhaps, that lies behind the bull's quizzical smile.

"Luminosity, darkness, broad space, and the contrast of colour have been linked to profound themes such as tragedy, ecstasy, and the sublime..." Whether the base of a Berwickshire cliff or the sand-sprawl of Tentsmuir or a hidden bay on a skerry-strewn shore of west Mull, the autumn sights and sounds of a colony of those seals we call the Atlantic grey live up to that assessment of Mark Rothko. But it is the Tentsmuir landscape that pays truest homage to his art.

◎ ◎ ◎

Late lunch at Crail in the early September sun was based on one of my simplest of food philosophies. If you're going to eat seafood, eat it where they catch fish. At Crail's too-picturesque-for-its-own-good harbour (every Scottish calendar photographer since the dawn of photography has paused here, most more than once) there is a wee wooden shed that sells live lobsters and dead crab rolls. I sat on the harbour wall with a fresh coffee and a fresh crab roll, re-ran the morning in my head, and the uncharted months of autumn that lay ahead, and all was well in my world. Few things taste of the sea the way fresh crab does, and what with that and the salt air and the coffee and the sun on my face and a few still-lingering terns gatecrashing the sea a few yards offshore with all the style of an Olympic medallist and twice as much grace, and a headful of seals, I was in no hurry to go anywhere.

Ahead lay the inland drive back to the edge of the Highlands, the land-locked heartland of Scotland, and whenever I go to my native coast and have to drive back west again I start cross-examining my motives, and wondering why the hell I don't return to where I unquestionably belong. Still looking for answers.

◉ ◉ ◉

Driving back among neat and gently contoured farms, I stopped to watch a ploughed field. The earth here is an exquisite shade of deep red-fox-red and the lowering afternoon sunlight ennobled the art of the ploughman, for it burnished the crests of the furrows and shadowed the depths. The fall of the earth from crest to shadow was briefly immortalised. I wondered what the ploughman Burns might have made of it. There is a Gaelic word for the swathe of earth turned by the plough – *sgrìobh* – but as far as I know Lowland Scots has no equivalent. I sense a missed opportunity, for there is no denying the artistry of the endeavours of a good ploughman when the soil he has to work with is as textured and toned as this. There should be a word that arose out of its own landscape to acclaim the result.

The ploughed earth had a further embellishment, for it was starred by hundreds of black-headed gulls that had just floated up from the sea and now waded the crests and troughs of these earthen waves and trawled the invertebrate shoals of the soil. I had been watching for about twenty minutes when a hefty buzzard (a female, I guessed from its bulk) crossed the low skyline of the next field and put every gull to flight. The buzzard is more of a small mammal predator than a birder, and in any case a gull is probably a level or two above its pay grade, but that eagle-shaped silhouette against the sky is an ancient enough symbol of adversity to activate the ritual of the first line of defence among flocks of grounded birds, which is not to be a sitting duck. Clustered fliers in large numbers confuse the predator and the manoeuvre tips the odds in favour of the prey species. The buzzard crossed the ploughed field without pause or deviation while the gulls swirled loudly above. In five minutes all was restored and the gulls gleamed gluttonously among the furrows.

A yellowhammer started calling from the topmost sprig of a hawthorn hedge. I like yellowhammers, like their poise and their vivid here-I-am bravado that fires to a particularly rich canary shade in sunlight. The species does have a specifically Lowland Scots word of its own – *yellayite* or just *yite* – which I also like. It may not possess the musical prowess of canaries (its single phrase is repeated *ad infinitum* bordering on *ad nauseam* and ends in a strung-out metallic *ziinngg!* as if it was constantly surprising itself), but something in the moment made me reach for a pencil and a notebook and a sketch of half a poem spilled over the paper, and I have just found it again.

And oh the yellow light
And the caller air

And the yellayite zinging
On the wire there, bright

In autumn-leaf-yellow-and-brown
And thistledown

One day I'll finish it.

◎ ◎ ◎

These first savours of autumn in such a tranquil and Lowland landscape are little more than dropped hints of the season to come. Mostly the trees are still green here, the hedgerows still flower, and when the first week of September is as warm as that particular week had proved to be, the second-and-third-brood nesters of the bird world are still fetching and carrying. It is only in the late afternoons and early evenings that the change is palpable – the deepening, cooling, yellowing of the light, "and all the air a solemn stillness holds". The atmosphere heightens, and, perhaps especially in a nature writer on a mission to pin down the nature of autumn, the senses are briefly supercharged. My westering journey was arrested again by an unkempt roadside acre wedged between two fields and in which a handful of young trees had been planted. Among them were a yellowing maple and (so close to it that their leaves overlapped and the illusion of flames in a hearth was irresistible) a dark-crimson-leafed sweet chestnut. I took a few photographs, then, because I liked the look of a sunlit-and-shadowed wood across the road, I walked back to where I had left the car in the entrance to an old earth track that led into the trees.

I was wearing light shoes with thin soles, and had not bothered to change them for the boots or wellies that live permanently in the back of the car. So I walked carefully into the wood for a while, watching where I was putting my feet, but then reverted to type and began to walk looking upwards, because upwards is where the glories of an old woodland usually lie (and notwithstanding the green woodpecker of Glen Finglas), which explains why I inadvertently trod on some acorns, felt them press uncomfortably into the soles of my feet, and so disturbed a long-dormant shadow that would return to haunt my progress through autumn with its old darkness.

Chapter Four

The Unexpected Eagle

THERE ARE FEW PLACES I know better or set out for more readily than Balquhidder Glen. It used to be in the old county of Perthshire but, without moving one inch, in recent years it has drifted into (so the road signs say) "The District of Stirling" and into the Loch Lomond and the Trossachs National Park. I think of it as none of these things but rather as a kind of still centre of the Southern Highlands. It is a well-wooded east-west glen that wilders as it westers until its single-track road stops in its own tracks at Inverlochlarig, the end of a cul-de-sac memorably furnished with elegantly sculpted mountains – Stob Binnein and Stob a' Choin.

There is a quality of softness about the particular beauty that pervades these hillsides, lochs and hidden side glens, one that is immediately absent the moment you breast the watershed on the north side of the glen and stare north to a spreadeagle of mountain landscape that grows ever harder-edged into northern distance. That quality fosters a wider diversity of wildlife that harsher Highlands lack. I lived nearby for some years; my windows were full of its charms.

My particular way into the hills climbs through forest, mostly spruce, some larch. Birches and rowans (their leaves already flecked with yellow) flourish anywhere they can find a toehold. Handsome, limb-flexing, broad-crowned, deep-dark-green Scots pines gather loosely under the mountain, as historically significant a reminder of the old order of this glen as the Ring of Brodgar is to Orkney. In the dense shadows of the spruces, frost had crept out onto the track in the night and now as the sun began to warm the morning after, the unmistakeable tang of the dawn of one more new autumn seasoned the air.

Two ravens started calling to each other in the pines and from three trees apart, and a fluke of their rocky hinterland threw echoes at me, so that echoes and real-time voices overlapped again and again over several minutes. Ravens are always worth watching at the best of times but here, when they give loud and frantic voice, it can mean they are discomfited by the presence of the neighbourhood golden eagles, so I stopped and scanned the glen with binoculars, because the eagles were why I was in the glen. For years, I was involved in an organised watch on their eyrie to counter the worst excesses of egg thieves. In the course of those years I became a willing apostle for the gospel of eagles. What had been an enthusiasm weaned on the masterworks of Seton Gordon became a crusade. "It was a long time ago – April, 1904 – since I photographed my first golden eagle's eyrie," he had written in 1955, thirty years after his first golden eagle book, and he was still writing about them twenty-two years later just before he died in his nineties. My idea of a role model. I never shared his passion for photographing from hides the intimacies of eyrie life, never enjoyed being in a hide at all, but his writing had stirred something in me and my mission became to try and understand more about the eagle's life *out there* on its territory, in flight, for in flight is where the nature of the bird reveals itself. In my book *The Eagle's Way* (Saraband, 2014), I wrote:

> *I started to watch eagles being eagles. These were no longer the chance encounters that every mountaineer knows, but rather they were the direct consequence of the fact that I was looking for them with eyes wide open and a new thrill in the back of my throat. In the course of two or three years I also lost any interest in climbing a mountain to reach the top. Instead I was lured by eagle-thraldom into a different relationship, first with the mountain world then with all wild landscape, a relationship whose objectives became the unravelling of nature's secrets, a better understanding of the wild world.*

Eventually the spruce forest relented and the glen opened into its high alpine-meadow-like upper chamber, a kind of box canyon dignified by a mountain birchwood. The grass was knee-high now and still green, albeit a faded green, a jaded green. The high mountain grass had begun the same process that coloured the oakwood, the leaves have given up on chlorophyll. A few weeks hence, and for a few mesmeric days, the floor of the upper glen would be orange, as would mountainsides all across the land, the earlier the further north, like autumn itself. A few late marsh orchids were still in flower, and grass of Parnassus (loveliest of all mountain flowers) basked in the sunlight. Grass of Parnassus is *Fionnan Geal* in Gaelic, and one little field guide I know translates it as "pleasant little pale one" and I suppose you cannot say fairer than that, although I can't help thinking that Gaelic is a more accomplished language than that.

But mostly I was watching the sky (unclouded Californian blue, but paling to white only in the north above the headwall), the three sides of the skyline and all their buttresses and trees, and especially I scanned the middle distances, which is the hardest part. "If you want to see eagles," Mike Tomkies told me more than once (and he was another accomplished champion of golden eagles), "you must learn to scan the middle distance." I duly learned, and he was right.

I know the eyrie ledge, at least I know where it is, I have never set foot on it. There are rules about these things. I know the ways the eagles come in to the eyrie, I know some of their favourite perches. But by early September, the young have flown, if they have had young this year. Their track record is not particularly good. Much of my spring and summer had been spent furth of here and no intelligence reached me via the grapevine about their nesting season. The simple way at this point in the year is just to spend time in the glen and up on the watershed with long views over the eagles' territory and see what turns up. And I am well versed in the art of dealing with the disappointment of the many days when nothing turns up at all. Over the years of the organised watches I had all the views of golden eagles at the nest that I could ever wish for, and now I mostly avoid the nesting season altogether. In *The Eagle's Way* I wrote about my ambition to become a part of the eagles' landscape and to be accepted as such, and that remains the be all and end all. Two things induce eagles to desert the nest: a protracted, cold, wet spring and human disturbance. I can do nothing about Highland weather, but I can remove myself from whatever accumulation of human disturbance comes their way.

But even when eagles don't reveal themselves, there are no dull hours in the glen. I found a young peregrine falcon against the sky, one of this year's, autumn-shaded, and much more prone to hovering than the adults. They can all do it, but seem to discard the idea when they discover how fast they really are. There was a kestrel up on the watershed too, and which hovers for a living, copper in the sun, fan-tailed, flicker-winged. There were red deer stags crossing the west skyline high up, moving from shadow into sunlight, girding their loins and growing sleek and ready for the imminent rut, when their voices will provide the mountain anthem of every Highland autumn. But I was seeing no eagles.

I was dawdling back down through the upper part of the glen, following the burn for a while, enjoying the sun. The walk back down through the spruces would be in shadow, and quite a few degrees colder. I stopped to watch some small trout in a pool, and just as I began to rebuke myself for my lack of knowledge about fish, a crow started to call. At first I was more absorbed in the fish and the voice only half-registered. Then, as it kept on and on and on, I decided to pay it some attention. The problem was that I couldn't see it, for it was hidden behind the spruces to the south-east. There is a high crag over there where I have seen eagles before. If the crow was there…

But, of course, as with ravens in such a glen, so with crows. The voice was stationary so the bird was perched, and its persistence suggested at least the possibility of a perched eagle either on the crag or in a spruce. The other possibility was no eagle at all and a crow that liked the sound of its own voice. Back on the forest track I pounded down through the trees to a place where I could see the crag, the crow, and whatever else it may or may not have on its mind. Halfway there, it fell silent.

When a sightline finally opened up, there was, inevitably, no crow to be seen and nothing else to confirm my suspicion. But crows and eagles can cover distance in no time at all when they put their mind to it, and it seemed worthwhile hanging around for a few minutes. Then a rock just below the skyline decanted a large bird I had simply not seen, and which promptly disappeared over the skyline. The thing to remember about a skyline is that it is only a skyline where you are standing. Climb up or down and the skyline changes. Beyond this one there lies a broad hill shoulder where a golden eagle might hunt, and if it was hunting there it might reappear just as easily as it disappeared, and especially if it decided to gain a bit of height. Then I heard a raven.

It was the raven that appeared high over the skyline, and perhaps a hundred feet above the crag where I thought the crow had perched. It dived down, giving voice, disappeared behind the skyline and reappeared almost at once in a steep climb. This was more promising. Not for the first time in my thirty-something eagle-watching years, I saw the eagle shadow before I saw the eagle, for the sun had

planted it out on the open hillside before the eagle emerged
from a small gulley just below the skyline's rock outcrops.
What followed was snatches of the confrontation, infuriat-
ingly brief and distant even for good binoculars.

The eagle climbed as the raven fell, the eagle in silence,
the raven falsetto-croaking to the rhythm of its wingbeats. But as the eagle climbed, something in the way it
was flying gave me pause for thought, for it seemed to be
making rather hard work of it, huge air-swatting wingbeats with wings almost vertical at the top of the stroke.
It didn't look right. Then there was a moment against the
sky's deep-blue cloudlessness when the two birds were no
more than a few feet apart, and at that point I took the
first of two photographs with a camera that was hopelessly
inadequate for the purpose, photographs which I knew
would be hopelessly blurred, but they might just confirm
something. I have the equally inadequate result before me
as I write this, and I have blown them up on the laptop
screen to the point just before the image disintegrates
entirely. There are the eagle's wings almost vertical, the
further one hidden behind the nearer one. The raven's
wingspan is at its fullest extent, and it is barely as wide as a
single eagle wing. The other unmistakeable characteristic
that confirmed what I wanted to know was the huge size
of the eagle's beak in relation to its head. It was unquestionably a young sea eagle.

In the two years since I wrote *The Eagle's Way*, I have
often wondered when this might happen, when sea eagles
might begin to find the Balquhidder landscape to their
liking. That book's proposition was that ever since the

reintroduction of sea eagles on the east coast of Scotland, and birds from there began to find their way right across the country to the established west coast population around Mull, a kind of two-way, coast-to-coast highway had begun to evolve between the Tay estuary and Mull, and that through fraternising with young sea eagles on their travels, the golden eagles too had become travellers along this same highway. What I did not know at the time was whether this was completely new behaviour or very old behaviour indeed that had lapsed with the demise of the sea eagle, but now the circumstances had begun to recur that made it possible again. As time goes by, I am more and more convinced that the latter is true, and that as more sea eagles cross the country in both directions, they are attracted back into historic sea eagle landscapes by the presence of golden eagles there.

In every respect, Balquhidder Glen is perfect sea eagle habitat, and in *The Eagle's Way* I described an encounter between the established golden eagles and a wandering sea eagle several miles to the north, beyond the watershed and down in Glen Dochart, which had always seemed to me to be the northern limit of the golden eagles' territory. But the setting of this new encounter was in the golden eagles' heartland, and if it has been around for a while, there must have been some spectacular face-offs during their nesting season. My own experience has been that if such face-offs happen in the air then the golden eagle can outfly the sea eagle every time, but if they happen on the ground, say around the carcase of dead deer, the sea eagle can out-muscle the golden.

Over the next few days, as I prepared to head north to the Isle of Harris Mountain Festival and to catch up with old friends on Skye, I wondered often what had been going on in this glen I know and love so well while my back was turned.

Chapter Five

Skye: A Love
Durable as Gabbro

THE OLD SNOW is a metaphor for the mountain. It has its
river valleys and marshes in the sodden surroundings fed by
its leaking meltwaters. It has its fringing forests in the alpine
plants and mosses which flourish in its shadow and by its
grace. It has its corries in the scooping sculptures of heat and
rain. It has its plateau where you can step from rock on to
snow and know the ground no less firm beneath your feet.
It has its bedrock in the oldest snows at its heart which may
never melt, where even this sun has not won through.

Jim Crumley
A High and Lonely Place
(Jonathan Cape, 1990; Whittles Publishing, 2000)

THERE WAS OLD SNOW on the north face of Ben Nevis as I
drove beneath its blunt bulk at the tail end of a crawling
caravan of traffic. On my countless pilgrimages to Skye, it
has always seemed a long haul through Lochaber. I lowered the window for a better view and raised a hand in
acknowledgement of the colossus and its snow that had
survived the summer, and who knows how many before

that. The Ben is not my favourite mountain. I've never climbed it, and I can't imagine why I would want to now, although I've looked up at it from the summits of all its neighbours. I've never liked sharing a mountain with hundreds of other people at a time, and The Ben, being the highest, attracts more than its fair share of nutters and nincompoops as well as harmless Munro-baggers bagging the ultimate Munro (the bagging thing never got under my skin either). But its sheer size in a Scottish context and its relatively inaccessible nooks above 3,000 feet create the most favourable conditions outside the Cairngorms for old snow patches to survive, some through many a winter.

Every August since 2008, the Royal Meteorological Society has counted – and measured – patches of old snow on Highland mountains. Just before I set off north, one snow-patch enthusiast had posted some details about The Ben online. He said the "most permanent" patch of snow in the Lochaber area had been there since 2006 "and this year it was huge". It extended up the mountain from around 3,400 feet to 4,200 feet, and would have been about fifty feet thick at the centre. So that one is going nowhere any time soon.

As I changed down to third behind a motorhome behind a truck loaded preposterously high with what I assumed was cattle fodder, I felt a sense of rightness about the high snow's sudden appearance in the early stages of my mission to pin down a sense of the season. The quotation at the start of this chapter is from my old book about the Cairngorms, and it was written one September in the late 1980s after a hot late summer. Earlier in the same chapter I had written:

For eight weeks, the Hill has panted through the longest days, cooled only in darkless night, but in a deep and slabby gouge of red rock a twenty-feet-thick wedge of tunnelled snow still limpets against the mountain. It was that kind of winter, but up here it usually is. I see in the old snow the old mountain, a small symptom of what Nan Shepherd, poet of these hills, called "the total mountain". Only the snow can speak to you of winter in high summer, stir in you the four-season awareness which I hold as a prerequisite to my understanding of any landscape. I like to let my mind linger over a day such as this, then, from its zenith, pitch the same landscape headlong into winter, conjure a huge December moon to glitter down on the ice-bloated grasses at my feet...By harnessing such extremes of the mountain's climate and character to a single train of thought, I widen the breadth of awareness, the range of disciplines I try to bring to bear on the landscape. The exercise's reward is a deepening understanding, the prising free of the Cairngorms' most elusive secrets...

It all seemed a good omen for a nature writer in the early days of a new adventure about the richness and the diversity and the various savours of wildness that attend the march of our seasons across the face of our land. I raised my hand to the hoary old mountain again, closed the window, settled back in my seat, stared at the gleaming white gable end of the campervan, which bore (in flowing italics picked out in vicious silver) the legend "Auto Dream Maker", and I turned up the volume of the Karen Matheson disc in my CD player. After a short pause, the supreme voice of my country's native singers began to caress the lyrics of the Gaelic air, *Chi Mi Bhuam* – "I See Afar". Good omens abounded.

⊙ ⊙ ⊙

I ate my lunch on a rock on the shore of Loch Oich. The hills around the loch are darkly over-spruced, and rendered dull as a result. In the great panoply of crimes committed against nature by my species, I consider that turning a hillside dull in pursuit of economic policy is one of the least palatable. At Loch Oich that day, the forestry industry's bacon was saved by a level tier of beech trees that caught the sunlight suddenly and flared into deep yellow life, the yellow slowly seeping along the shore as sunlight cleared a path through cloud. Then I saw that the water was playing the same game but upended in its quieter reaches, so that two bands of fire – one on the lowest slopes of the hills, the other paralleling it in the water – spread slowly across the small portion of the West Highlands laid out in front of me. Again and again among the quieter moments over the next few days, the phenomenon nudged its way back into my mind. I remembered talking to a member of staff at the local computer shop in Stirling when some (to me) inexplicable infestation afflicted my laptop. As I watched him wield his virtual scalpel through the wretched thing's innards, he said that half his working life was spent watching bands of green or blue travel across a screen. The next time I see him, I must remember to tell him about my two bands of yellow fire. Only autumn can do this, and yes, it IS a magic trick.

Driving north, one more essential truth about early autumn presented itself. It is that its particular palette drifts slowly down the country from the north, and that with the aid of time-lapse photography, it would probably be possible to measure its speed of travel. Why anyone would want to is another matter.

I turned off at Shiel Bridge for Mam Ratagan and the ferry at Glenelg, which has been my preferred way of boarding Skye for forty years. The crossing of Mam Ratagan is an agreeably strenuous driving experience, intermingling hairpins and extreme gradients with the occasional thrill of meeting a fully laden forestry truck coming the other way. It helps if you know that you are about to change planets. Beyond the crest the way west softens slightly to long, swooping downhills and your first eyeful of the Isle of Skye. I found autumn again in the flat-bottomed glen of Moyle, neatly folded away in the shape of compact fields of palest gold and rusty brown. The road forks at Glenelg, left for the village and the long, slow road down the coast to Sandaig (Gavin Maxwell's immortal Camusfearna), but I slithered away right for the ferry. I have had my share, and arguably more than my share, of encounters with Maxwell's ghost on that ultimately ill-starred acreage of turf and bejewelled islands bounded by the Allt Mor Santaig. I have made arguably too many years of pilgrimages there in pursuit of some will-o'-the-wisp of my own creating, but it was born out of a sense of debt for all that his writing galvanised in me. At its most unsettling, there was this, which I wrote in a long-forgotten and long-extinct little book called *The Heart of Skye* (Colin Baxter, 1994):

It was, if such a thing exists, a God-given day. It was as though nature had paused in that early September no-man's-land between summer and autumn and meshed into a golden lull that was neither of them. All the strewn fineries of the land wore their finest seductions, a bazaar of nature, "the golden Skye bird" sunned its crooked wings and the Sound of Sleat was a sash of creased silk. From the smoky skin of a first frost on my tent at dawn until the last snuffed sunset flame, Maxwell's world held still and quiet, a day harvested by nature for herself.

I sat alone in its midst, my mind rummaging through Maxwell's life there and those traits of my own life which had lured me there and now lured me back. It was then that I became aware of three silhouettes across the bay, black against the gold glare of light, a man, a boy, and what looked like an awkwardly running dog. They paused at the bay's furthest edge and the sound of the voices carried clearly across the stillness, although I could make out no words. I grew vaguely irritated at their presence because it had stemmed the free flow of my thoughts, even at such a distance. When I am alone in such a place I like to be alone there.

The three figures passed briefly out of sight behind a low rise in the ground and I watched for them to re-emerge beyond it. They did not re-emerge, nor did they re-trace their steps. After a few minutes I crossed to the place, mild irritation tempered by unease. There was no trace of anyone having been there – no sound, no footprint, no swimming figures in a square mile of sea, nothing. The thought lodged, and it remains neither accepted nor dismissed, that the "awkward dog" was an otter. There was a time on that shore when the

silhouettes of a man and a boy and an otter walking together
would have been as familiar as the rocks and the sand and
the curve of the burn. Weeks later, I would discover that I
had seen my phantom ten years to the day after Maxwell's
death. I felt as if he had tapped me on the shoulder.

Eventually, the faintly obsessive nature of these "pilgrimages" dawned on me and suddenly I found them distasteful, and most certainly out of character. I am content now to pick up one of a handful of my favourite Gavin Maxwell books and reacquaint myself with the crafted prose and its occasionally startling poetic turns, the vivid water-colour word-pictures of landscape, the glowing moments of nature, the humour, the melancholy.

◉ ◉ ◉

The Glenelg ferry, *Glenachulish*, was tied up at the pier and there were no waiting cars. The two ferrymen were having a break and a coffee at the top of the pier. One signalled me to stop as I threatened to drive down on to the boat. Never argue with a ferryman. I parked and stepped out and said hello. The skipper was politely chatty for a while, but he grew enthusiastic when I asked him about Victor and Orla. Victor and Orla have become Internet sensations over the last few years, ever since they set up home just up the hill there and began strutting their stuff before the incredulous eyes of ferry passengers. Victor and Orla are a breeding pair of sea eagles. Why oh why do people give stupid names to wild creatures?

The gist of the skipper's chat was that the male was

there daily when there were chicks to feed, June and July were best. Now he was elsewhere; Loch Hourn, the skipper thought, but he didn't know why. I told him my guess was this: the waters of that mountain-strewn sea loch are infinitely easier to feed in than the chaotic waters of the narrows, but it would be a long haul to carry a hefty fish or a sea bird back to the nest from the loch; whereas from here, once the fish is snared, it's the shortest of short hops back up to the nest. And maybe that's why he fishes in Loch Hourn once the chicks are fledged.

The skipper looked at me directly for the first time, considered me for several seconds with a silent stare and an expression as hard as gabbro, and I thought for a moment he was going to put me in my place with a well-judged rebuke. Outsider. Mainlander. (East coast mainlander at that.) Tourist. Smart-ass. I imagined that he would be accustomed to visitors hanging on his every word and not cluttering up his story about his waters and his eagles with this quite uncalled-for intrusion with its nonsensical theory that I had concocted in seconds. Or there again, he could have been weighing it up to see if there was anything in it that might embellish his story for the next stranger who wandered down the slipway with a chestful of binoculars and a camera with a telephoto lens the size of a baseball bat. But if he thought any of these things he was too polite to voice them and he turned away again and nodded to the blunt bulk of the island across the water, and in the slow, salted speech of the Hebridean he said that this year 7,000 people had used the wee hide built over on the Skye side by the Forestry Commission and the RSPB. He said he thought the eagles were good for business, at which point he rose to his feet, nodded towards my car and walked down the slipway to make me briefly a part of his business too.

◉ ◉ ◉

Beyond Kylerhea on the Skye shore, or rather above Kylerhea (because from the islander's point of view there is no "beyond" at Kylerhea for the solitary road stops where the ferry starts, and beyond that is mainland Scotland where the world becomes something other)...so, above Kylerhea is where the Mam Ratagan's evil twin lies, only it is wilder, the gradients markedly steeper, and the drops markedly longer. Welcome to Glen Arroch. Halfway up, a male hen harrier flashed across my bows, a poem in silver-grey and black with that diagnostic scrap of brilliant harrier white at the top its tail. Its shadow-into-sunlight starburst was the most distant of echoes of the green woodpecker in far-off Glen Finglas. But bird-watching from a car on this, the west side of Glen Arroch, is not a serious option so I swore softly to myself and promised to stop at the top, where the road crossed the watershed, so that I might scan the slopes below on the off-off-chance that the harrier was still there, slow as thistledown and one-yard high, searching for vole tremors or a passing cloud of finches on the move. Then with that streamlined absence of fuss that is the badge of all its tribe, it might soar fifty feet, bank and turn in its own length and tilt the whole mighty seaboard of the West Highlands through forty-five degrees in the process. Were it not for game-keepers, who mostly harbour a profound hatred of the bird, I would imagine being a hen harrier must be a lot of fun.

At the watershed I breasted the very last rise and the world burst apart. Where there had been the confining edges of Skye and Scotland at the narrows far below (the Atlantic trying to cram itself into not much more than a quarter of a mile), and after that the hemmed-in devilry of the ascent of Glen Arroch, suddenly there is laid out before you a panorama of Skye's greatest hits, most notably that mountain masterpiece of the Gods of Celtic legend – the Cuillin, attended by their coast-to-coast retinue of lesser mountains and hills all across the waist of the island and all of it happed and patched with sunlight and the fast shadows of clouds. I stepped out into salt-laden wind and ocean-brightened sunlight, and it occurs to me now (and only now as I write this) that I had forgotten all about the hen harrier.

The heather on this flank of the hill had been blasted into bleak-midwinter-brown submission weeks before, and there was hardly a wild flower in sight. I found a way of sitting in the deepest heather so that most of the wind was deflected, ate a hardening sandwich and drank the lukewarm dregs of the coffee flask while I feasted my eyes. I have been coming to Skye for more than forty years and at every season of the year, but mostly in autumn and most of those autumn visits in September, and this is why. That pale-flaming sea and ocean-wide sky framing the dark blue herd of Cuillin summits and their black-shadowed corries that finally charge down the flank of Gars-Bheinn into the sea where the ocean-going pancake of Soay sits just offshore and forever in their thrall. This is gabbro's finest hour. Then there is Blà Bheinn, their so elegant semi-detached neighbour; then the Red Hills then the sleek bulk of Beinn na Cailleach, which does for the village of Broadford what Gars-Bheinn does for Soay. Beyond these, a second tier of mountains, the Red Cuillin that curve their airy, writhing, scree-bitten, pale-pink-granite ridge from Glamaig to the pyramidal wonder that is Marsco. There is no getting accustomed to that parliament of mountains and every time I drive up Glen Arroch from Kylerhea they reform in my mind and I prepare for that first glimpse just beyond the last rise, and it is always more than I remember. Many Septembers ago now I sat here or hereabouts on just such a day, and I scribbled down the following in about ten minutes, what Norman MacCaig would have called a one-fag poem:

Love Durable as Gabbro
Walk with me, there is a shore
where love buoyantly drowns out
the ocean's dirge.

Sail with me, there is a tide
love boards to blur
the horizon's distinctions.

Fly with me, there is an air
wherein love dances
among balletic eagles.

Climb with me, there is a mountain
where love durable as granite
weathers all storms.

◉ ◉ ◉

Isle Ornsay is the other Skye. It huddles in the lee of an east-facing slope and stares out across the Sound of Sleat. I found it drowsing in the late afternoon, the tide edging towards high, a marauding posse of twenty red-breasted mergansers cruising the lee of the lighthouse island, the punk-rockers of duck sub-culture. I think they were designed by Lego. What else explains a long, thin, scarlet bill, a glossy, bottle-green head with a quiff of quills at the back, a dog collar, a flamboyant chestnut breast that segues into black towards the back, the black adorned with white patches like naval epaulettes, then the long, slim, taper-ing body and folded wings of black and white and grey? Either that or some mad biologist's laboratory experiment had crossed a cock pheasant with a black-throated diver. Their jerking heads appear to be tugging the rest of their reluctant anatomy along, rather in the manner of those oil-rig supply vessels that have all the superstructure at the front. But underwater they are as lithe as otters and lethally efficient in the matter of inhaling small fish by the shoal. I rather like them.

Isle Ornsay and I go way, way back. An image of its lighthouse island with the Knoydart mountains beyond smote me with something like an electric shock of longing the first time I thumbed through the pages of *Raven Seek Thy Brother*, the third of Gavin Maxwell's Camusfearna trilogy. The intervening volume (and it does rather inter-vene), *The Rocks Remain*, was something of a let-down for my young self after the kind of impact that *Ring of*

Bright Water made on me, but *Raven* was full-throated and muscular, from the curse of the rowan tree to the final fulfilment of that curse, the complete destruction of Camusfearna by fire. The photograph of the lighthouse reignited my response to *Ring of Bright Water*, not because it was a good photograph – it wasn't particularly – but because it synthesised in a moment the possibilities of such a life in such a landscape. I would become in my head a writer of landscapes, a seeker after landscape imagery, a quester in pursuit of nature's secrets in a Camusfearna of my own choosing. To write my own *Ring of Bright Water* was and still is the *raison d'être* for giving up a reasonably lucrative career in newspaper journalism more or less twenty years to the day after I first saw the photograph. All this surged through me as I parked by Hotel Eilean Iarmain, the Isle Ornsay Hotel, and walked back a few hundred yards along the single-track road to a point where I could – yet again – put the lighthouse in its frame of mountains, and align it in aesthetic juxtaposition with Beinn Sgritheall. I took new photographs on a new camera, then I just stood and stared and stared. Here I was on a journey through autumn that I had envisaged as being a new kind of writing exploration for me, and here I was back on the shore of Isle Ornsay with Gavin Maxwell's writing on my mind.

At a time when his income was, by his own admission, "indecently large" the Northern Lighthouse Board had automated the local lighthouses of Isle Ornsay and Kyleakin on Eilean Bàn (on which the Skye Bridge now stamps one of its imperious feet) and he decided to buy both – none

of which did anything to diminish my fascination for Isle
Ornsay, although I should also insist that I fell for its many
charms purely on my own merits. Nevertheless, it did not
hurt that Gavin Maxwell had written that no view, other
than perhaps his first of Camusfearna, had "affected me as
strongly as the splendour and the purity of the immense
panorama spread before the islet...It was as though I had
found Camusfearna once again, the same sense of sudden
freedom and elation." He dreamed out loud that he might
live at peace again "in a limitless bubble of blue water and
blue air...here one might set back the clock and re-enter
Eden". As it happened, it would be the Kyleakin Light on
Eilean Bàn to which he turned and where he lived the last
years of his life. I always thought he had turned his back
on Eden then.

I found something else in my old Skye book, *The
Heart of Skye*. It was published in 1994, when I could
write: "I have travelled addictively to Skye for twen-
ty-five years, a hundred times by now, but I have not
yet learned to live there. It could be that I never will.
Skye's cause has not been greatly assisted by most of its
incomers. Skye does not need me as much as I need
Skye." And twenty-one years further on, that perceptive
little thought is no less true.

The arms of Isle Ornsay's W-shaped bay shut out all
Skye and funnel your gaze to the island and its lighthouse
and cottages and beyond to the Sound of Sleat and inevitably, as if compelled by some magnetic impulse, to the
tranquil overlordship of Beinn Sgritheall. The southern-
most shore of the bay contains all that in a suggestive

curve, suggestive that is, of a pathway towards the promise of the landscape beyond the funnel, persuasive as a full moon at the window or a voice in a dream. Once, on an old autumn visit to Sandaig, I had pitched my tent further down the coast. Long after dark, and under a sky of more stars than I have ever seen from one place before or since, I walked the beach listening to the sounds of the October night, and especially curlews, oystercatchers and the rough-edged discord of the red deer rut. I realised eventually that quite apart from the challenging volleys amid the stags up the mountain above my tent, challenge and counter-challenge were also reverberating across the Sound of Sleat. I have heard the rut in many arenas, and been over-intimately surrounded by it in a Cairngorms pinewood, but it has rarely thrilled me as it did that night of stars.

Sleep hardly entered into the night's equation, and at something like 5a.m. I gave up the unequal struggle, packed a breakfast for later, and set out in the pre-dawn darkness to climb Beinn Sgritheall. I had no clear idea of the easiest route, and it certainly would not have started from the Sandaig shore, but I went straight up for as long as that option was a practical proposition. Strenuous physical activity took over from the night's too-strenuous mental activity and put wings on my feet and power in my legs and oxygen in my lungs. I never climbed a mountain that way again. I had certainly never done it before. I paused after the first hour, looked round, and saw Loch Hourn in a trance, a glimpse of a landscape of dream. The water was a milky cream tinted the most fragile shade of lilac that the merest notion of the word "pastel" allows. The Knoydart mountains, now with Ladhar Bheinn for a centrepiece, might have been hewn coal, almost too black to be convincing, like a stage set. Nearer the base of the mountains the water darkened to turquoise, but still with that milky opacity. I long since took a vow of abstinence in the matter of trying to write down sunrises and sunsets, having decided that the dash through nature's palette is fit work for gods but not for writers. But every now and then the climber paused and turned and gasped, then turned again and climbed on.

I found my way round the mountain to the upper reaches of the Allt Mor Santaig, the mountain burn that feeds the waterfall that Maxwell called "the soul of Camusfearna", then ripples in a glittering arc to the sea, an arc that became – in a certain light – a ring of bright water.

The mountain grew bare as I kept the company of the burn. Towards the summit it flirted as much with the underworld as the overworld, disappearing beneath the rocks for yards at a time. The nightcap of cloud that the mountain had worn under the stars, began to evaporate, and revealed a snowcap underneath. At last, in the very summit rocks, I found the place where the Allt Mor Santaig issued out of the ground for the first time, almost as much ice as water. I filled a small bottle to unite with the bottle of Talisker I had left in the tent. If the burn fed the soul of Camusfearna, then here was the womb that begat the soul. I patted the summit cairn at 8a.m. and had breakfast.

SKYE: A LOVE DURABLE AS GABBRO

All that wandering year
I walked by waters:

Spring was the Allt Mor Santaig
weaned at Sgritheall's breast,
still mad with summit snows
as it tried to sweeten the sea.

Summer I swam among islands
sunned and lulled by enchantment's distance,
blind to the warning light a-flicker
on Eden's shore.

Autumn a dark and troublesome river
among fiery rowans; spates
plucked away one luckless tree,
still blazing.

Winter an ocean grey
on grey with fast storms,
water at its utmost. There
where I walked

along the frayed edge of the land
I found a honeyed stream
lapping with bright tongues
at all that oceanic salt.

It was the Allt Mor Santaig
a year older but no wiser.

For me, Isle Ornsay is two shores. One is the bay with its mergansers, otters, herons, curlews, island, and a grainy black-and-white lighthouse in thrall to a mountain. The other is the shore beyond the funnel, the further limit of a "limitless bubble of blue water and blue air", that shore where Beinn Sgritheall towers primeval and protective over a far lighthouse at the seaward end of a chain of small islands, a curve of white sand, and a ring of bright water, all of which serve – among many other things – as a memorial to a life defined by a landscape in which, among all its torments, it found a brief era of peace.

◉ ◉ ◉

Broadford Bay was brim full and blue at slack water, but a blue tinted yellow and lilac, and there was a strange green bar right across the visible sea in the north. The forecast for Harris in the morning (and the ferry crossing of the Minch) was a troubling cocktail of wind and rain, but for the moment the gods of storm held their breath, and I stepped out from dinner in my hotel to find the land swathed in a repertoire of the most profound stillnesses. An hour before, the edge of the bay was clustered with midges, the last of the summer swine. Now, thanks to one more benevolent influence of burgeoning autumn, the air was layered with an energising chill. No other time of year moves so effortlessly between tee-shirt warmth and fleece-chill in the time it takes to shower, eat a lasagne, and renew old acquaintance with a pint of Red Cuillin.

Every skerry had its heron, was possessed by its heron. There are many more herons than skerries hereabouts, so whenever a new arrival drifted down from a small conifer copse on a croft, and on wings held in a downward curve, and with disproportionately skinny legs dangling optimistically in search of a perch, it was inevitably driven off again at once by the heron in possession of its two square yards of rock. So harsh, so abrasive, was the rebuke from the skerry owner that it left a scar on the agreeable nature of the bay's evening, like a skate blade on clean ice. It seemed excessive.

I sat on a rock and scoured the bay, its near and far waters and all its shores, rocky and wooded. Where were the otters, the sea eagles? The township that straggles prettily along the east shore of the bay bears the un-Hebridean name Waterloo. It is a cul-de-sac, a one-car-wide road to nowhere (just ask Napoleon). Beyond, paths of varying degrees of certainty cross bogs and machair and yield to shoreline rock. I have followed them eagerly for years. I watched two roe deer, a doe and this year's calf, nibbling at God-knows what in the bog until the doe caught my scent and stared long and hard, and the calf went and stood by her flank. I was sure she would run and command the calf to follow, but she did no such thing. Instead, she walked a dozen yards until she reached a wind-blown, salt-stunted willow about as tall as I am myself and as wide as it was tall. There she stopped and the calf stopped with her. She had deliberately put the tree between herself and me to break up her shape, and to demonstrate that she knew more about her territory than I did, and was infinitely more streetwise in the deployment of its advantages. And now the calf knew the trick too. If I had crossed the moor without seeing the deer move behind the tree, if the deer had been there all the time, the chances are I would have seen nothing at all beyond a singularly unexceptional willow tree. This was new behaviour to me, but I suspect it is very old behaviour for a savvy roe deer.

That night I dreamed of lighthouses and mountains with old and new snow patches.

Chapter Six

Twenty-four
Hours on Harris

HARRIS HEAVED INTO FOCUS as the ferry barged through the
final onslaught of short waves whose crests were whipped
off by a sour north-westerly. A gannet seemed drawn to the
boat, a moving cliff of possibilities. Nesting responsibilities
would be over. This one could have been on an away-day
to Harris from St Kilda, forty miles out into the Atlantic.
The gannet's long-winged stride devours distance. During
the nesting season, round trips of 500 miles to the feeding
grounds are not unusual. Forty miles is an hour's cruise at
wavetop height. All kinds of birds are forever making that
journey. When I was on St Kilda for two weeks in 1988
researching my first book, among the birds that turned up
were a golden eagle (almost certainly from Harris), four
incredibly scruffy turtle doves (from God knows where),
and a cock snow bunting.

The gannet inspected the boat from every angle, from
stem to stern, and from waterline to bridge. In the glasses
it looked as white as sunlit snow against the many greys of
ocean and island landfall. My good omen bird. But as the
MV *Hebrides* slowed to ease its relatively ponderous bulk
through the rocky wiles of Loch Tarbert, the gannet all

but stalled above the stern, dropped a starboard wingtip and glided away from her on unbeating wings through a huge arc that dropped towards the sea, where it straightened and levelled out inches above the surface to resume its fishing foray among the dark east coast bays of Harris, a foray which the arrival of the *Hebrides* had interrupted. The only land in which it has any interest of any kind throughout its life is the square yard of stinking rock that accommodates a sitting female and her egg.

The entrance to Tarbert, the island's only town, demands that the ferryman executes a sustained gentle curve. The moment recalled the skipper of a small eagle-watching boat out of Ulva Ferry on Mull on which I had had a memorable sail three years before (see *The Eagle's Way*). He was a droll man in English and Gaelic and in his practised commentary and off-script conversations with passengers (though I imagine that from one boatload to the next they ask the same questions). I heard one woman ask, with a hint of wonder in her voice:

"And do you know every rock along this stretch of coast?"

"No I don't…" – pause while she took this news in – "but I know all the places where there aren't any."

Knowing the places where there aren't any and putting your boat in them is, I further imagine, what sailing in Hebridean waters is all about. When your boat is the MV *Hebrides* and the all-purpose lifeline between Harris and Skye and thereafter the rest of the world, there is arguably a little more to it. Actually there is a lot more to it, for she is 5,506 tonnes, ninety-nine metres long, her draught is

3.32 metres, she is 15.8 metres across the beam, and she can carry 612 passengers and ninety cars. And it's not as if mooring offshore is an option. She must berth alongside in Tarbert so that she inches into the vehicle ramp with the ease and precision of fingers in a cashmere glove. The rocks glide past wondrously close, and never at any stage from my vantage point leaning over the rail on the top deck does the feat look possible. That it is possible and happens routinely seven days a week is surely mostly because the skipper knows all the places there aren't any.

I turned away to look out at the island. After Skye, Harris looks unfinished. Its rock skeleton still grows, so that it bursts through what is clearly an inadequate covering of vegetation. Evidence of autumn at work and far advanced was everywhere and ubiquitous as rock. Even under the colour-sapping burden of such an oppressive and sodden grey shroud, it looked as if the whole island had been brushed with a thinly applied patina of rust.

I drove from the belly of the MV *Hebrides* the few hundred yards to my hotel, checked in, deposited my overnight bag in my room, turned round and left the building. I had a handful of hours of wind-fretted, rain-soaked early autumn daylight before I had to prepare for a talk about eagles at the Isle of Harris Mountain Festival. I pointed the car towards the west, to maybe the best beaches in the world. It had been a long time, and as I drove I realised that I had forgotten the jolt-in-the-solar-plexus impact of the Harris landscape on unaccustomed eyes. This would be my third time, the second had been at least twenty years ago, the first about ten years before that. The place is a ribcage, a geology of broken bones. Rock heaps up like crouching armies, and here and there it infiltrates the edge of the road where you drive, as if it rather disapproves of the idea of tarmac and is hell-bent on reclaiming it. One day, I have no doubt, it will succeed. Nothing is flat, nothing straight, nothing tame, nothing domestic. The land itself is dark, and yet it accommodates a savage species of beauty. More than anything else, Harris is its own place, and the entire repertoire of Scottish islandness knows nothing like it.

I don't like treating islands this way. It strikes me as disrespectful. I would be here for not much more than twenty-four hours, do my job of work, sleep, and tomorrow make what I could of the few hours at my disposal, and it appeared they would be seriously circumscribed by a hostile weather forecast. But the least I could do was to pay the island what respects I could, beginning half an hour after I had landed.

What is not rock is water. There is heather and there is half-hearted grass that seems to be perpetually pleading for mercy from the weather or being eaten by sheep, and the trees are rarer than milestones and they have given up pleading and they are low and wiry and bent because the salt-smothered wind insists on it. But mostly there is rock and there is water: lochs, lochans, pools, burns, and fast, fitful and slender rivers; and sea lochs so long and languorous that they are tidally indolent at their heads, much to the delight of sudden hundreds of birds. Knee-deep in shallowest of shallows are the wader tribes – lapwings, golden plovers, redshanks, greenshanks, and curlews towering over them all like a tribe of Gullivers among Lilliputians. The shock is the clarity of the water (I had forgotten that too), and where it languished over the pallor of sand and even at a distance, the legs of every bird were clearly visible underwater.

After crossing the island from Tarbert, the first of the west coast beaches appeared to my unfamiliar eyes like a cold mirage or a landscape in a dream or a glimpse of Tír Nan Óg (which I had always assumed would be much further west than Harris), or just an out-and-out miracle. First the ocean appeared, and on such a day it was grey on grey and darkening towards the almost black line of the horizon, but then the road fell away in front of me so that the inshore ocean and its startling sprawl of sand drew an audible gasp, and seeing was barely believing at all. And that suddenly deep, deep green ocean with a mysterious blue undertone (where did *that* shade derive from under such a ponderous greyness of skies?) edged the whole towards turquoise but never quite got there. And the low coastal hills in the north were purple.

Enchantment set in where the final – the only – breaker unfurled. I had anticipated an ocean in a rage that reflected the weather, and the intemperate crossing of the Minch, but instead I met an ocean in a dwam. The breaker, having broken, advanced on the shore in a low, wide band the white of new snow, and in the form of a perfect arc. Ahead of it, between its leading edge and the shore, there were three more arcs that fitted the white water and each other with all the precision and perfection of rainbows. The first of these was a pale greyish blue, the next a line of white as thin as a lace, and that marked the last reach of water up the beach. But the tide was newly turned, so there was a fourth arc, a yard wide, and it wore the lightest dusting of lilac, and that was damp sand that showed where the sea had newly departed from the high water mark.

And yet the chief glory was the sand itself, a pale blaze of sand, especially on such a day; not white exactly, but after Skye, where the few scraps of sandy beaches are black-ish, these were so exotic I felt entitled to expect palm trees. And they were so unbesmirched, so perfect, so untrodden, it was as if the ice age had just finished the day before yesterday and the provider of sand, following everywhere in its wake, had just finished the west coast of Harris, and no creature – neither bird nor mammal of two legs or four – and no camper van, had found the place yet.

Travel south down the coast and beaches imbued with that same surreal quality of organic mesmerism keep materialising round the next corner, until finally the road swerves away south-east and the bemused traveller is done with his dalliance in Tír Nan Óg. I spent hours with notebook and camera, writing in the rain (use a pencil!), and photographing (as I saw it) Rothko-esque compositions with horizontal bands of sand and ocean and sky in thirds and fifths and sevenths. And after all that I found a rock and sat on it and poured coffee and stared and marvelled and soaked it up. Sometimes you get days, or rather moments within days, when something parts or slips aside – like a screen or a door you never saw before – and what lies beyond is nothing less than an intimate exposition of the lie of the land. Confronted by such a moment, my response is always the same – look at it, listen to it. Such thoughts that cross my mind then are elemental and huge and soon I put them down again and settle for thought-lessness and the free rein of instinct, for all smaller thoughts are impossible.

⊙ ⊙ ⊙

I had been asked to talk to the Isle of Harris Mountain Festival about eagles following the publication of my book, *The Eagle's Way*, which concerns itself primarily with a swathe of land clear from the Tay estuary to the Isle of Mull, its slowly increasing sea eagle presence and the golden eagle's response. I had been vaguely uneasy that some islanders might have detected a coals-to-Newcastle tendency, given that Harris and neighbouring Lewis have good populations of both eagle tribes. As it turned out, the unease was completely groundless, and besides, I had already rationalised my approach to myself, and to the Harris audience. In a country the size of Scotland, no community of distance-devouring eagles can exist in isolation. For example, a wandering sea eagle from the Tay estuary that travels west and arrives on Mull has reached not so much a destination as an eagle distribution hub that lays out the entire western seaboard at its disposal, from the Mull of Galloway and the Mull of Kintyre to the Butt of Lewis, Cape Wrath, and beyond even to Orkney, where 6,000 years earlier men and sea eagles had such closely co-operative lifestyles that they were buried side by side in the same tomb, the so-called Tomb of the Eagles. My book's story begins there, and in the second chapter there is a detailed account of the first sea eagle I ever saw, on Mingulay, which is a few links down the chain of the Western Isles from Harris. And Harris is now writing its own chapter in the glittering success story of the return of the native. Two of the more remarkable of my friend Laurie Campbell's photographs that grace *The Eagle's Way* are the fruits of his long-term fascination with the wildlife of Harris. And it is fair to say that by now all Scotland is once again a realm of eagles: every mile of coast knows its eagle shadows, and as with my notional eagle highway between the Tay estuary and Mull, wandering sea eagles are finding ready company among wandering young golden eagles and some are luring them on forays furth of their Highlands and Islands strongholds.

Sitting in the hotel bar with a nightcap whisky, an open notebook, and a head full of the events of an extraordinary day that had begun with a pastel dawn over Broadford Bay, I thought I might find one more insight and write it down. An hour and another whisky later I called it a night. The notebook page was as untroubled as the sands of Luskentyre.

◎ ◎ ◎

The next morning the weather had turned really dirty. The wind was up and the wee burn below my hotel bedroom window had developed a hoarse anger in the night. I had a few hours before lunch and the afternoon queue for the ferry back to Skye, and decided to spend them on a leisurely exploration of the C-road to Roghadal at the south end of the island. Sunday morning on Harris is q-u-i-e-t. Of the island's 2,000 souls, more than sixty per cent are Gaelic-speaking and the Sabbatarian philosophy is still alive and well. I would go softly down through the island along one of the most beautiful, bold, brass-necked, berserk roads I have ever travelled. It also marked the moment in this book's journey when I met full-blown autumn head-on and saw the morning's storm ram it down the landscape's throat.

Such a blasted landscape as now unfurled before me had clearly no memory left of even the latest of late summer. This salt-scented gale hurdled the crests of the smaller hills then dived down what had been leeward slopes yesterday, there to feed and whiten the burns into instant waterfalls. These were suddenly as thick on the ground as a gentler landscape might accommodate trees. I swore some of these burns were not even there yesterday, but most of them rumbled over rocks and tossed stallion manes of white water arcing into the air so that they tumbled heads over their own heels and spent themselves, exhausted, among chains of hissing lochans whose occasional sheltered shores (usually under an overhanging black buttress or beneath a wind-cheating gorge) were thickly layered with flowerless water lily pads. In high summer tranquillity (I brought the most outrageous stretch of my imagination to bear on rec-reating that lost scene) they must have been as exquisite as they were outrageous. *Water lilies! HERE!*

I had the road utterly to myself, and whenever possible I stopped by the ends of sea lochs and the edges of inlets (the road helpfully swerved and dipped down to water level to greet every one of them and embrace the high-tide rocks) to scan water and shore in the less than optimistic pursuit of even a glimpse of another of nature's creatures other than myself. There was not much chance of birdlife picking morsels out of the teeth of the storm, and if there was to be anything at all, the chances were that it would be raven, for it takes the vilest of weather to ground a raven, and such is its inclination to fly in the face of storm, I suspect a hint of masochistic endeavour lurks deep within that likeable blackguard. The thought had barely registered when I negotiated one more blind summit, with a lethal hairpin built in, to be confronted with two ravens in the middle of the road about a dozen yards away reducing a few bloody inches of meat and fur to a sodden pulp. They accorded me a two-second appraising stare, giving me (as I fancied it) the benefit of the doubt that I might not actually run them over, but even at my Sabbath dawdle they were simply too close. One flew left, the other right (and the morsel of whatever it had been flew with that bird). I was able to pull the car off the road a few yards further on, and when I opened the door to look back, both birds and their bite-sized snack were back on the road, and they were sharing it amicably. They behaved as if I was not there.

I like ravens. I found myself wondering if they responded to life in a more or less treeless landscape the same way their Icelandic kin do when it comes to sourcing nest material and nest sites. I found a nest there on a glassless window ledge in an old outbuilding. The nest was built entirely with little pieces of barbed wire fence instead of twigs, but it had the most sumptuous lining of sheep's wool of any nest I have ever seen.

The rest of that little expedition, I saw only two other birds, a meadow pipit and a stonechat. What I was really hoping for on the water was otters. Otters are indifferent to weather and the east coast of Harris is pretty well perfect for them. And while this stop-and-start morning was diametrically opposed to my preferred otter watching methodology, you just never know. Sometimes, right time, right place, is all you need. But mostly, nothing was moving at all. Blackface sheep hunkered down behind rocks, at the bottom of banks, under bridges, in the doorway of a broken shed, in the lee of outbuildings, diggers, tractors, vans and in the ditch beside passing places, though all they were passing was time. They are the last survivors of a doomed way of life, for there is little interest in shepherding left among the islanders and even less money. I am no fan of sheep (their capacity to wreck landscapes and their historic symbolism as an instrument of Clearance get in the way), but on days like this one, it is hard not to admire their stoicism, at the very least.

Below one croft house, down at the water's edge of a long, quiet and deep-sided inlet, a small dark brown horse and a slightly paler donkey stood motionless and shoulder to shoulder under the imperfect shelter of that rarest of Harris phenomena – a willow tree. Two hours later, having been to Roghadal and back, I passed them again and neither had moved an inch.

In the long, lifeless lulls of the morning I reconsidered the road, wondered idly if there could a more torturous man-made object on earth. The shortest of straights felt like mistakes, as though an opportunity to throw in an extra gratuitous hairpin had been wilfully spurned. It gathered in un-numbered and still skinnier roads, coastal cul-de-sacs every one, tributaries to its own chaotic mainstream. I wondered at the townships it visited, wondered what the inhabitants do (the ones that live there, that is, as opposed to the second home owners and self-catering holiday letters), for they can't all be crofters and artists and postmen and nature writers.

One more blind summit flipped into a bend round a small buttress. The whole island is more or less a conglomeration of buttresses, some of which gather into wondrous 2,000-feet mountains (not that I would see them on this trip, but I remembered). Whatever their size, they are all parties to a dark-toned conspiracy hell-bent on out-witting the weather and on clothing the island with its rare strain of savage beauty. There was a brief lessening in the rainfall's volume. I slid down the driver's window, the better to execute one more sideways glance at one more seaweedy bay, and there was an otter staring back at my passing glance from where a tiny shrug of the Atlantic Ocean heaved a few inches of orange tangle up the flank of a low, flat-topped shoreline rock, a rock with an otter on top; then the ocean sucked and the orange drapery subsided.

There was – of course – nowhere to stop. The road demanded that I rounded the buttress, where I judged that a patch of roadside was wet rock, not bog. It turned out to be both, but at least there was no ditch. My car is small and light and blessed with very good four-wheel-drive. This is why. The car and I took our chances, we did not sink, but I jumped out into a bog.

Two minutes later I was clamped to the side of the buttress, being flayed by the wind and stared at by an otter with one forepaw pinning what looked like a lumpsucker to its rock. Its other front paw was raised, a gesture with an interrogatory edge, like a pet dog cravenly quizzing its human about the possibility of Bonio. We were twenty yards apart and I was twenty feet higher. If anything, I was wetter than the otter, and certainly colder, but right there, right then, there was nothing I would rather be doing, nowhere I would rather be doing it. A primitive connection fell into place. A thin thread bound us – otter and otter-watcher – to that moment, that crossing of paths in that most elemental of landscapes. Hail fellow, well met.

⊙ ⊙ ⊙

The MV *Hebrides* crept out of Loch Tarbert in the late afternoon, assiduously adhering to the places where there weren't any. She spun round to face the Minch and the disturbingly corrugated waters. It would be a crossing sponsored by Stugeron. The more open water the *Hebrides* put between herself and Harris, the more the island seemed to recede back into itself, and to darken to almost black while its hills snored through the Sabbath shrouded in a collapsed sky the most hodden of greys. It was not how I wanted to remember Harris. I sought out a quiet corner of the lounge for a while to try and write down something of the morning. Strange, I thought, how ferryboat coffee always tastes like bilgewater. Half an hour crept past, but my mood of darkness was a contagion I had brought aboard from the island and I seemed to have been incubating it ever since. I was like Burns's sulky, sullen dame:

Gathering her brows like gathering storm,
Nursing her wrath to keep it warm.

The miracle, when it happened was as sudden as whirl-winds, as startling as rainbows. It began in the south. A far headland of Skye appeared where none had been visible moments before. A hole appeared in the dark smother of cloud, and sunlight poured through in a tilted column that smote the headland and lit it from stem to stern. It was the precursor of a kind of Hebridean rebirth that made all the visible world new again. The sky fissured open and began to leak sunlight with the energy it had recently channelled into leaking rain, and in a hundred different places at once. The ocean that had been dull grey was suddenly ablaze, then slowly turned deep green and deep blue, and an unbroken band of molten white light as vivid as a Luskentyre breaker lay all along the horizon.

Ahead, Skye basked. Astern, Harris smouldered. Other islands sprang up all along the western skyline to resume their accustomed positions in the ocean. The air filled with birds. The effect among the passengers was to galvanise them out of a huddle of torpor. Voices were raised, extended hands and arms pointed out the bleeding obvious, eyes squinted, sunglasses appeared, cameras and phones gorged on the spectacle like gulls on a dead whale. The mood of everyone and everything was transformed.

Arriving at Uig on Skye and driving up the hill on the road south to Sligachan and the rest of the world was a thing of constantly unfolding and expanding marvels, an instant festival of distance. At the summit I stopped in a lay-by to let the ferry traffic breenge on by. I stood outside the car, felt warmth on my face, heard swallows and martins, and the sense of having changed planets for the second time in twenty-four hours was utterly, utterly complete.

Chapter Seven

South-making

IT WAS THE 18TH OF SEPTEMBER. When I am at home in Stirling my day often begins with a round walk of about three miles for newspapers and coffee. The route varies between well-treed suburban streets and the edge of an old half-mile long fragment of estate woodland with resident buzzards, sparrowhawks, an occasional peregrine, tawny owls, and an impressive array of small birds. Fox, squirrel (grey, alas), roe deer are there too, and I keep hoping for badgers. The footpath alongside the wood is dignified by circular copses of whitebeam, maple, silver birch and rowan, and a beautiful line of a dozen larches, which were nicely poised to strut their autumn stuff.

That morning was the first that autumn when I saw leaves fall freely from a windless tree. Job done. Almost at once, the sound of pink-footed geese drifted over the morning and I found them much higher than I had expected. There are swifts in the street from late spring to late summer, and as soon as the sight and especially the sound of them is gone, they leave an emptiness in their wake, which is only redeemed by the arrival of the geese. The fields of the Carse of Stirling both east and west of the city hold big numbers of pinkfeet and greylag and a scattering of Canadas, and these cruise low above the roof-tops and the watercourse of the River Forth, back and forward all autumn and all winter, as do small skeins of mute and whooper swans. The arrival of the pinkfeet heralds this happy association between those particular bird tribes and the place where I live.

I heard the geese, I looked up, found them, and then checked the date on my newspaper, which is how I knew it was the 18th of September in the first place. I shook my head in disbelief and I may have muttered aloud:

"The old bastard! I don't believe it."

There was this old keeper I used to know a little bit. He was a friend of a friend, or at least the neighbour of a friend, and our paths would cross in a wee country pub a few miles away. He had no time for me, which was fine, because I didn't like him one little bit. He used to trot out these old country sayings about the first cuckoo and the last swift and the first snow on the nearest mountains and what a good crop of rowan berries signified, and many, many more from the fortune cookie school of countryside lore. And he used to insist that year after year after year, the first pinkfeet turned up at his local loch on the 18th of September, and God help us all if they didn't. He was a cantankerous drunk. He was also cantankerous sober. He was the kind of old school unreconstructed Victorian keeper whose idea of demonstrating his good stewardship of the estate where he worked was to nail a pair of hen harrier wings to a barn door every now and then. He tended his gibbet with particular zeal. He was also an old-school countryman, the kind who believed that the golden age ended the day before yesterday. In fairness, what he did not know about the wildlife on his patch was not worth knowing, but he seemed to kill most of it anyway. His favourite word was "vermin", which he articulated like a spit, with the present participle of a four-letter word before it, and the curl of a lip by way of an afterthought embellishment. He's long dead, and it is a long, long time since I gave him a moment's thought, and it never troubles me from one year to the next to check when the geese return. I don't worry about such things, and confine myself to being content that they do return.

But then there was that morning and I heard them and I looked up and they were too high to be cruising between fields, and I thought that this was probably their arrival, and then some old stoorie corner of my mind struggled sluggishly into life and coughed up that particular foible of his, so I looked at the date on the newspaper in my hand and it said it was the 18th of September.

⊙ ⊙ ⊙

All was south-making. Something was astir on the land. One morning the highest fairway on a golf course in the Stirlingshire hills was a-blur with skylarks. Two, three hundred perhaps, feeding on grass seeds, drifting on, feeding again, drifting on, always heading in the same direction, like tumbleweed. And the following afternoon I climbed halfway up the flank of a small glen to find that processions of swallows and house martins were whirring past the edge of the hill. Their thin voices drizzled down the greying afternoon air, although the hint of threnody I heard was all in the mind.

An hour passed, and still they came in sporadic clusters, scraps of puny daring hell-bent on the Med, Africa, wherever the weather suited their clothes. I wished them a silent *bon voyage*, and thanks for cheering the spring and summer with their long-gone kindred spirits, the swifts. I urged them to watch out for men with raised guns and nets. It is the most baffling of rituals, birds shot or trapped are sold pickled in jars around the Med. Who thinks that is a worthwhile trade? Worse, who pays for a jar of skylarks, and presumably eats them? Do they think it will help their singing voices?

Migration blows my mind, whether wildebeest or warbler, eel or Arctic tern, swan or swallow. Not to go is not an option. The command is heard – south! Or it is seen, or felt, or tasted on the north wind, but somehow it manifests itself, and clouds of birds or handfuls of butterflies take wing, align themselves to routes as old as life on their portion of the planet (and some are tutored by their parents and some make it up as they go along), and they make common cause with rivers of travellers, because that's life.

So I sat and watched the procession pass. That small glen bounced the soft rain of their voices between its low crags, splintering echoes all afternoon and possibly all morning too, for I had only arrived in time for a late lunch. Then suddenly the thing was done. Suddenly there were no more birds. I looked over my shoulder. The air was empty. The glen was stilled with a kind of gentle mourning. Not the mourning of death but of that departure which is mitigated by the certainty of return. I do not think that it is fanciful to ascribe such knowledge, such awareness to the land itself. For the life of the land is one of seasonal ritual, of arrivals and departures and passing strangers, of warmth and blizzard. The land is everything, the be-all and end-all. In a million different ways every day of every year, wildlife registers its appreciation of the land where it nests, dens, mates, feeds, hunts and travels. It is an arrogance bordering on tyranny to assume that our species knows better than nature what is good for the land. We need to listen to the land, and there is no better season than this one, when so much unfolds that is natural and wild and the land supplies food for the travellers, landmarks for the journey, destinations. If we as a species cannot recover the art of listening to the lost speech of the land, we are on a short road to nowhere at all.

◉ ◉ ◉

And then there was the kingfisher, a final grace-note flourish on the very last September morning.

Long before the concept of book festivals was invented, William Hazlitt (1778–1830) cautioned: "An author is bound to write – well or ill, wisely or foolishly; it is his trade. But I do not see that he is bound to talk, any more than he is bound to dance, or ride, or fence better than other people. Reading, study, silence, thought, are a bad introduction to loquacity. It would be sooner learnt of chambermaids and tapsters..." He makes a fair point. There is no reason why writers should make better talkers than, say, taxi drivers, some of which are interesting, some boring, and some never shut up. Happily the book festival business turned a deaf ear towards Hazlitt's warning.

Wigtown, being Scotland's booktown, is very good at book festivals. It is a very Scottish little town on the edge of a huge and beautiful bay on the Solway coast of Scotland's far south-west. This also means that it is a particularly good book festival for a nature writer; many of the locals know a lot about the subject because of the way it laps around the foreshore of their everyday lives. So I was in Wigtown on the last day of September, and just when nothing could possibly be further from my mind, there was the kingfisher. I had a couple of hours after breakfast before my event, so with my friend and festival colleague Polly Pullar, I strolled down in breathless low morning sunlight to a bird hide on the edge of the saltmarshes that fringe Wigtown Bay. The tide was at its lowest ebb, exposing a remarkable landscape of glossy, grey-brown mud around the old harbour, its quiet river and a peculiar little dead-straight cutting that jutted inland just below the hide.

After a few minutes enlivened by the appearance of a young peregrine falcon that stirred something of a panic in the wader flocks, I heard a thin, piping bird voice I knew I should recognise, but sometimes, if the context is wrong, I can be a little slow on the uptake. Then, into unclouded sunlight and glittering like something improbable by Fabergé, a kingfisher swept in from the river and up the cutting, where I lost sight of it below the bank. But moments later it reappeared and perched on a piece of broken wood that lay in the throat of the cutting, and there, for half a minute, it sunbathed, surrounded by high banks of that elephant-coloured mud, which served only to intensify the kingfisher kaleidoscope and to heighten the notion of a bird in a dream. I heard Polly's voice mutter: "A kingfisher, encased in a sunbeam!"

It flew back to the river and vanished, but the sense of a visitation would linger all day. It was time to go, time to try and allay Hazlitt's misgivings once more.

Part Two

October

Chapter Eight

Daylight on the Dream

THE SUNLIGHT IN THE AFTERNOON that first day of October had a quality. Wherever it shone directly on to the trunks of the trees, wherever it negotiated its way through the slowly thinning canopies of hundreds of oaks and their sporadic underlings, the rowans and the hollies, that I could see without turning my head, wherever it lit a long and ragged-edged strip of forest floor or a grassy clearing a dozen yards wide, wherever it fell on the darkest bark and blackest roots, it struck notes of bright white in them all, notes so vitally defined that I felt I might hear them. Any moment, the oakwood might resound to the silvery voices of vibraphones or woody wind chimes, and every note would sustain and ripple and hang on the air in layers of tremolo echoes. Their pitch would change every time a sliver of a breeze wafted a holly spray so its shadow shifted on an oak trunk, beginning new notes, silencing old ones with its prickling dance.

I became aware that I was walking very, very slowly, military-march-slow but without its insistent rhythm of ostentation, "pibroch-slow" I said aloud to myself and smiled at the memory of Finlay MacRae playing the *Desperate Battle of the Birds* in the pinewoods of Glen Affric.

I have seen cock capercaillies in just such terrain, treading with the same dignity and certainty and strut, and I saw a man embody both landscape and bagpipe music and make them an indivisible and organic whole, and I had never seen it done before and never seen it done since, and forty years after the event I can see him slow-slow-slow-slow-slow marching as he played. I was a young journalist at the time, just beginning to flex my muscles on environmental themes, and something I had written about forestry produced an invitation from the Forestry Commission to meet Finlay, who had just won an award from the American Society of Travel Writers for his work on native pine-wood restoration. That day in Glen Affric, there were half a dozen journalists from a variety of newspapers, but as the music moved like smoke through the trees, and as it rose and fell through the careful ground-and-variations structure of pibroch, I was the only one with tears in my eyes. I shook his hand afterwards, but I couldn't say a word. He smiled and nodded and put a hand on my shoulder. To this day, a good piper and a great pibroch puts me in mind of Scots pines and capercaillies.

Twenty years later I would discover that we had a great friend in common. His name was Pat Sandeman, whose life evolved around three passions – birds, Gaelic and piping. His day job had been in the family wine and spirits business. He was much older than I am but late in his life we became great friends and he would recruit me as his "eyes and ears" on various birdwatching missions. One day he mentioned Finlay MacRae, and I said: "The piper?" "Yes," he said, "why, do you know him?"

So I told him the story of our Glen Affric encounter, and from his pocket he produced a letter from Finlay he had received that day, and it was clear from the odd paragraph he read out that they were great friends indeed. Pat had been, by his own admission, a "ropey" piper, whereas Finlay, by international agreement, was a genius, and a pupil of one of the greatest of all piping tutors, the Head of Army Piping at Edinburgh Castle, Pipe Major Willie Ross. But, as I was about to discover, so – very briefly – was Pat. He told me this story.

He had tried and failed several times to get an interview with Willie Ross, then he got "an introduction", and I fancy I now know who had done the introducing. They had talked for a while at the Castle, and eventually Ross had said he was just too busy and didn't have room for Pat. Then, as he was leaving, he asked Pat what line he was in. Wine and spirits, said Pat. A pause. I think I might just be able to squeeze you in, said Ross. He was duly squeezed, but struggled to make headway. One day, making "a right hash" of a pibroch during a lesson, Willie Ross had stopped him in his tracks and said:

"No, no, no, you're playing it all wrong. You'll never be a great piper. All the great pipers are dead, and to tell you the truth, I'm not feeling very well myself."

◉ ◉ ◉

So that was why I was smiling to myself as I realised how the mood of these Trossachs oakwoods had infiltrated my mind and slowed my stride to the soft stealth of a Finlay MacRae. And I was walking along an animal trail not half a yard wide, and I knew by now that the trail builders included roe deer, fox, badger, red squirrel and pine marten, for I had seen all of them use it over the years and at different hours of day and night, and different seasons of the year. The trail wound between tree trunks and through clearings and spawned offshoots down to the river from time to time (all mammals must drink and most swim), and although I know the place as well as I know anywhere, it seemed to me that on that particular afternoon I could look at it with a new way of seeing. There was the sunlit wood and the shadowed wood and one was bright white and the other a deep ebony dark, and both were restless because of the movement of trees in the wind and the image occurred to me briefly of a kind of dance like the movement of chess pieces, and I wondered if this was how Ansel Adams ever saw woodland, and whether it explained his utter mastery of black and white landscape photography.

My favourites among his woodland images include one of aspens and one of redwoods, and in one you can see the sunlit gold of the leaves and their tremulous shimmer, and in the other the deep dark red of the bark and the colossal reach from soft ferny undergrowth to open sky, yet the achievement is rendered in shades of grey and black and white and the framing is tight and sunlight and sky are elsewhere, but the sense of what is not shown, and the colours of what is shown, are palpable. And I was looking at a sunlit wood and I was seeing in a kind of monochrome the essential elements that pinned it together and fastened it to its earth. And then, by setting something free that I could not possibly put a name to if I sat here and thought about it for a fortnight, I could allow in the canopy and the woodland floor and these were of fading green and paling yellow and darkening oak-leaf tans, and all of that gathered about me in such a slow whirl of pin-sharp detail that to write it down that way sounds dizzying. But its effect was the opposite: I had slowed and slowed without thinking about it, and then I stopped and I sat at the base of a sunlit oak with my back to its trunk and face to the sun and I felt becalmed, at rest and at ease with the wood itself. And this is how I go to work.

At various times I have been called a wildlife expert, a nature expert, a naturalist, an ecologist, a conservationist and disciple of biodiversity (I am none of these, I don't even know what the last one means and I also don't believe that it is possible to be "expert" in wildlife, let alone all nature, such is the limitless scope of the subject); nature is simply my preferred field, and when I go to work in its field, I go to write. And it has been my experience – and it still is – that if you go often enough and in an open frame of mind, and if you take the trouble to win a degree of intimacy with your subject whenever that allows, then there will be moments when you see something other in the familiar. All you have to do then is find a way to write it down.

An oak leaf fell on to the open page of my notebook. It was green and yellow and brown, and when I held it up to the light I could see many small holes and each one was haloed in sunlight. I put it back down on the page where it had landed and photographed it. I decided it looked a bit like a satellite image of Lewis and Harris, complete with their characteristic freckling of dubh-lochans. My habit of writing out in the woods, or in the hills, or by lochs and rivers and waterfalls and the edges of bogs, is fundamental to my ambition of effectively *becoming* nature, so that – however briefly – nature treats me as a part of the landscape. When I am sitting writing I am still and silent, and over the years all manner of things have landed on or chosen to explore the notebook in my lap. The majority of the leaves have been oak, but also birch, rowan, willow, larch needles and more robust bits of trees – acorns, pine cones, beech nuts, various catkins, twigs and, once, a piece of pine bark loosened by a treecreeper. Bugs seem to be attracted to its bright white glare with the blue ink doodles, especially butterflies. Once, I had just written down the words "they have more to fear from us than we have from them" (I think it was something to do with wolves) and had then laid the notebook aside on the grass for a moment, at which point a tortoiseshell butterfly landed on the page and its shadow fell over the two lines of handwriting, "embracing" it, or at least so I chose to interpret it at the time. Dragonflies have turned up too, as have ladybirds, pinewood ants (a marching column, too many for the comfort of a sitting writer; some of them carted off a sandwich crumb), spiders, bees, a burnet moth and, once, (and still the only bird) a robin, again while the notebook was on the ground rather than in my lap.

"Write in the very now where you find yourself," wrote Margiad Evans, "...there is no substitute even in divine inspiration for the touch of the moment, the touch of the daylight on the dream." I have quoted her many times, but nothing like the number of times I have been grateful for her priceless advice. How often, too, I have invoked her to myself, and that would include every time something of nature landed on my open notebook whether by accident or design; how often I wished I could have thanked her, how often wished our paths could have crossed, but she died (on her birthday) in 1958 and I was still a child, but a child of nature even then.

⊙ ⊙ ⊙

After ten days of high pressure and still, warm days, October finally cracked and threw a cloak of grey and rain over the woods and sent furious, scurrying salvoes of short-lived winds through the trees. There are few facets of nature I enjoy more than walking in the still centre of a wild wood while the winds torment the tree tops and set tree against tree as trunks are bowed against each other and limbs interlock amid thin screeches of protest. Deep in the oakwood and down near the river, I was stopped in my tracks by a broken runt of a tree I had never noticed before, but now it caught my eye because it was waving a crimson flag. It had been unexceptional as oak trees go, its girth was modest and it had forked at about seven feet high. What remained of the tree was the trunk, one limb hoisted from the fork at a shallow angle – about thirty degrees – and a skinny, broken-off branch where the rest of the fork must once have been. From the fork to the outermost broken tip of the surviving limb (surviving in the sense that it still exists, though it does not live) was perhaps another seven feet, certainly no more. The limb itself divided into two branches that had also broken apart but twisted rather elegantly and tapered to fine points. Much of the trunk was swaddled in thick moss, light and dark shades of green, but the scene-stealer was not of the tree, but rather a fly-by-night opportunist. Rooted in the moss and deadwood on the top side of the broken fork, a small cluster of stems of rosebay willowherb had rooted, and prospered, and now flaunted a pretty show of autumn-crimsoned leaves, conferring on the entire oak remnant a jaunty, rakish air that made me smile. I stopped to sketch it and take a few photographs. Moral: deadwood is the lifeblood of living woodlands, whether standing or prone.

Half a mile away in the same wood, a larger oak had succumbed to the previous winter's storms, crashed sideways across the path so that a new diversion was initiated, which navigated round the now vertically-realigned mass of roots that faced out towards the river like a huge, dark satellite dish with a hundred antennae. But the tree had declined to die completely. For although what had been its canopy was now smashed and bare, a frieze of around twenty leafy oak saplings a few inches high had sprung vertically from the horizontal trunk, and these made a kind of loose-knit hedge in shades of green and yellow and brown. I was looking at it from about twenty yards away when a great spotted woodpecker materialised on the very topmost claw of the upended roots, and from there dropped nimbly down onto the trunk and began to thread a tricky progress through the saplings with an ease that suggested this was not the first time. At any one time, the various components of its black and white and bright red plumage appeared through gaps in that inches-high screen of leaves, often revealing no more than the bird's head with its black crown, red nape and white cheeks, but other glimpses showed a bird apparently on tiptoe and craning its neck to see over the leaves. Once, in a bare patch of horizontal bark between saplings, it appeared to be discomfited, and stretched its entire body into a low-slung and elongated parody of a woodpecker's normally upright posture, and proceeded in tiny steps of its huge feet as if horizontal progress were an ordeal, and not a manoeuvre to be undertaken lightly.

At the far end of this unlikely journey, it astounded me by turning in its own length and retracing its steps. The point is that at every few steps it would pause and very clearly find food there, for not only was that dying oak tree determinedly fostering new oak life for as long as it produced any sustenance at all, but it was teeming with invertebrate life, and the woodpecker was not about to miss out, even if it meant having to improvise a new hunting technique. In dying as in death as in life, there is no more endlessly resourceful living organism than an oak tree.

Chapter Nine

In Memoriam,
James Anderson Crumley

I HAD BEEN WATCHING the pages of my diary advance towards the 12th of October, 2015, for some time. I had already decided what I would do that day but I had no means of knowing how the day would treat me. The Balgay Hill is one of two landmarks on the north shore of the Tay estuary, around which my home city of Dundee was built. The other, the Law, is higher, more conspicuous, more central and more famous, but the Balgay is mine. I lived the first eighteen years of my life on its slopes, thirteen of them in the prefab then five more in a new flat high on its east-facing slope with even more spectacular views of the Tay estuary. On the right kind of day, we could see the Bell Rock Lighthouse from one little side window, but the sitting room and the kitchen windows were full of the Balgay 200 yards away, and of the distant low hills of Fife that fringed the far bank of the upstream view of the Tay towards Newburgh. The Balgay itself is part wooded hill and part burial ground, and it is also there that my parents and three of my grandparents are buried, so one way or another its modest height and acreage has infiltrated my bloodstream, heart and mind since more or less day one.

For the morning of October 12th, 2015, I had hoped against hope for a perfect autumn day, in order to do the occasion justice. Instead, it was grey and windless, and tending towards drizzle, the trees of the Balgay smouldered rather than dazzled, and low cloud drifted in among the highest of them, blurring the edges of the most familiar hill shape of my life. The few geese whose voices I heard were lost in that low cloud. I felt somehow let down by the only place on Earth I have ever felt comfortable calling "home". This hillside that faces west over rooftops to the Tay estuary and winter sunsets is where I come from. My parents' grave is there, a quarter-of-a-mile as the grey goose flies from where our family prefab stood. That view upriver is as fair as anything in the land and the fairest by far in my personal anthology of my native landscapes, and if I could ask my father (I never did), I would imagine he'd say the same thing.

On the day of his funeral, the Balgay's woodland had worn its finest autumn clothes. As the cortege had driven along Riverside Drive, the Tay was a flat opal blue, and (as McGonagall had insisted) silvery. There were hauled-out seals on the sandbanks, cruising fleets of eiders, cormorants standing erect with their hands by their sides, the dark stillness of respect. A couple of old boys, Dad's generation or older, stopped near the Tay Bridge and turned to face the hearse as it passed; one saluted, as if he recognised the presence of an old soldier within.

After the family moved to the flat on the far side of the hill, he used to stand in the window and look out at an edited version of this same view to those blue Fife hills and almost sigh the words, "Ah, the bonnie hulls". It became his shorthand for favourite views of hills all across Scotland. The choice of vowel for "hills" is the Dundee dialect's preferred option, which he would slip into from time to time. They were bonnie that day as we had driven to the Balgay, and they were bonnie when we gathered round the grave. I remember little enough of the funeral other than the crowds (there must have been four or five hundred people; he was a much-loved, much admired man) and the lines of cars, the beauty of the day, and the intermittent and wholly appropriate voices of geese that provide the soundtrack for so many of my memories of the place. I found a letter not long ago that I had written to my mother a few days after the event that said I visited the grave five times the following day. I don't remember that either.

The Bonnie Hulls (by my father's grave)

"The bonnie hulls" — that sigh
was ever on your lips, your eye
on Tay's far shore, the Driesh
and Mayar, but here,
on Balgay's modest brow
we made you hillside.

Earth-to-earth's fate fit enough
but I'll have no dust-to-dust;
you left to my trust a legacy
I'll shine dust-free
until I can see

your face in it.
I'll cast your eyes
on Tay's far shore
and wonder evermore what hills
and rivers you've seen since
and in whose lugs
you cried them bonnie.

October 12th, 2015, was the 40th anniversary of that bleak and beautiful day. With the benefit of the intervening decades I now understand that I was not just mourning my father and his much-too-young death at sixty-three, but sorrowing too for what seemed like the end of my association with the first of all my landscapes. I was twenty-eight at the time, an upwardly mobile newspaper journalist living in Stirling and bouncing between jobs in Glasgow and Edinburgh, and there was a troubling finality about the day that felt like a kind of severance. Dad and Mum had moved, because of his health, to the far eastern edge of the city at Barnhill, and it was there that she lived for another eighteen years. The Balgay was no longer on the doorstep.

But at more or less the same time something else was astir, and that was the awakening of an environmental conscience that had begun to inform not just my more lucid moments of contemplation but also my journalism, and I began, tentatively, to flex my writing muscles in the cause of the holy grail of all worthwhile earth-writing – the landscape. As soon as that process began, so did a kind of restlessness in nature's cause, and I began to question its purpose and its sources. It is a process that still exercises me from time to time, and it coughs up more questions than certainties, but there is no doubting the wellspring. Many beautiful hills and shores and islands have lured me away from Dundee, but here remains the one place on Earth where that characteristic restlessness subsides. Here is where – more and more often – I return to draw breath, here is the place where I know best how to be still, how to *belong*. Landscapes are fundamental to what my life has become, the raw material for much of what my writing has become, a restless pilgrim for nature all across my own country and occasionally among a few of the wild north-ern places of the Earth. Here, among autumnal tree shad-ows on the Balgay Hill, lies the seedbed. This is where the boy with the goose-wonder in his eyes began to lay down a lifetime of remembering.

So forty years to the day since my father died I was in the Balgay. I thought I should mark it in some way and all that I could think of was to walk its familiar roads and paths and pause by favourite trees and sightlines, and linger over the memories they generated, and end up at the gravestone where I had already decided what I wanted to say. Then I turned uphill off the road and onto an earthen path with a few steps cut into it, and that was when – for the second time that autumn – I stepped on a smothering of acorns and felt them press uncomfortably through the soles of my shoes and into my feet. Here of all places, on this of all days. It is a feeling that reminds me of one of the worst days of my life. But first, I need to tell you a little about my father's father.

⊙ ⊙ ⊙

His name was Bob Crumley, and I have a cigarette card of him. He was famous from one end of Dundee to the other, and for a handful of seasons in the early years of the 20th century he was famous throughout the Scottish footballing world. He was the goalkeeper in a fine Dundee side that challenged for the league title and, in 1910, won the Scottish Cup for what is still the only time in the club's history. But he was also the black sheep of the family, and after his wife died of the Spanish flu epidemic in 1918, and while he was still away serving in World War I, his six children were taken under the wing of his dead wife's sister, and he had nothing whatever to do with them ever again.

Whatever the nature of the wedge driven between him and his family, whatever the pain and bitterness it engendered, it was smothered long since in a pact of silence or ignorance or both. He was never spoken about unless the subject under discussion was football. He was allowed his fame – it was undeniable – but he had been denied his humanity. My brother and I were told (by my mother) that he was a waster, a drunk, a womaniser, and that he was so despised that when he died there was no one to bury him and he lay in a pauper's grave in the Balgay.

And there the situation remained until one day in 1995 I decided to write a book about my home city, a homage to the place that I knew as I grew with it. It followed that, in the course of writing the book, there should be a chapter about my famous grandfather. By that time, none of my parents' generation was alive, so I began again with the bones of his footballing career, and then I decided to look him up in the obituaries section of Dundee's Wellgate Library. It took me ten minutes to find him and to discover that his funeral had been attended by 500 people, by the entire Dundee FC team of the day as a kind of guard of honour, and by three Lord Provosts of the city.

After that, it was clear that no family source of information was reliable so I went looking elsewhere and began to piece together a very different picture of the man. And I made a decision. It was that whatever the nature of the quarrel I wanted no part of it, I would be a broker of peace, I would find where he was buried, and put up a small stone. But first, I had to find the grave. I paid £10 for a death certificate, and armed with that and three different assurances that he was buried in the Balgay (though no one knew where), I was directed to a parks department office where I could have the certificate checked against a lair number.

That book I was writing became *The Road and the Miles* (Mainstream, 1996), and this is how I wrote down the sequence that ended with acorns pressing through the souls of my shoes:

"At least you have a date," said the man in the office. "We get people in here who are twenty years out." And he leafed through huge volumes of hand-written names, but not one of them said Robert Walker Crumley, and he lifted his head and said: "Well, he certainly isn't buried in the Balgay."

He patiently leafed through the other main cemetery files while I stood in a small and thoughtless vestibule in a mean red-brick building, surrounded by leaflets and brochures proclaiming the glories of Dundee's parks, while a garish poster incongruously proclaimed the tourist wares of Virginia, and both I and my naïve, ridiculous, solitary mission stood mutely in shreds. He came back shaking his head.

"Either he is buried in a churchyard, in which case you have a very difficult search on your hands, or, are you sure he wasn't cremated?"

Not now I wasn't, because I had been so sure he was buried in the Balgay. Cremation has never entered my mind. It was comparatively rare among working class folk in 1949. Then I remembered a letter I had received which named the local church where Bob Crumley had married his Jessie some years after his first wife had died, and which stressed her long association with that church. If there was a stone, perhaps there?

The road to Lochee (the tribal lodestone of the Crumleys for 120 years) passed a sign to the crematorium. I turned off on the impulse that would lead me to the knowledge I did not want to know. He had been cremated. There was no stone. The ashes had simply been scattered in the crematorium garden. The woman who imparted the information was a saint. Her manner was courteous and demonstrated unambiguously that she cared how the information would affect me. She brought the book, yet another huge tome of names, to the counter and read out the entry:

"Robert Walker Crumley, 4 Benvie Road, died January 27th, 1949, cremated on the 29th."

It was the woman's kindness more than any other single emotion which I took out into the crematorium garden. I had never walked in a crematorium garden before, never realised *that it would be full of substitute graves – trees, plants, flimsy plaques, benches. If there is a single moment in my life I would not wish on my worst enemy it is that one, that deluge of incomprehensible loneliness, that stupefying helplessness. I remember the press of strewn acorns through the soles of my shoes…and then I couldn't think of a single thing to do, nor a single place to go…*

You may remember that in Chapter Two I mentioned the two oak leaves and the one acorn and the three acorn cups that have kept me company on my writing table throughout the writing of this book. Every now and then, when the march of the words across the page pauses for breath or demands a fresh input of creative energy, I pick up the leaves and I think about the wonder of oak trees, and I balance the acorn back in its cup or look at it in the palm of my hand, where its more pointed end catches the light from the window the way a bird's eye glints with a speck of white light. I remembered interviewing a wildlife artist years ago who described the final moment of the painting when she put that white speck in the black eye as "sacred". I now understand what she meant.

I also understand now, after thinking about it often over too many years, that when I walked unthinkingly over the acorns in the Dundee crematorium, they were not pressing through the soles of my shoes at all, but rather my feet were pressing them into the earth, where some of them at least would become young oaks. Then I found these words in Hugh Johnson's matchless *Trees* (Mitchell Beazley, 1973; Octopus, 2010):

The Lammas shoots which make all oaks glow with new life in mid-summer show up most on a young tree. Last year one particular tree was so covered with new pink and golden leaves that no flowering cherry could have been more spectacular, and it took them six weeks to fade through pale green to dark.

So I have rescued the sanctity of oak trees from the impact of one bad afternoon twenty years ago, and I can resume my walk through the Balgay towards Dad's grave.

There's a road just inside the high stone wall that used to divide the Balgay from the long narrow strip of land that accommodated the prefabs. It was here that Dad taught me how to ride my first bike, walking alongside my precarious beginnings with one reassuring hand on the saddle, time after time, until the moment he removed his hand without telling me and suddenly I realised he was fifty yards behind me and laughing. I only fell off when I tried to show off by doing a u-turn.

The wall is still there. On the other side of the road is a wooded area that has been allowed to grow wild, and which I have become very fond of in recent years, in fact ever since Dundee City Council built a small cairn and erected a plaque to explain its meaning. It is Common Ground and it has been since 1870, and it exists to commemorate Dundee's unsung, unknown, unmemorialised souls, roughly 10,000 of them between 1870 and 2004. The unsung are commemorated here by great trees (including two Californian redwoods) and small, by saplings and shrubs and wild flowers, some of which tidy minds would call "weeds". Quiet paths thread these few acres, while above and beyond, the headstones of the sung and the memorialised stand in mown-grass ranks, and of course these include my parents and my three other grand-parents. But something in the rough-hewn cloisters of the Common Ground pleases and comforts me; that my old home city took the trouble to remember the unremem-bered and give them their place so that I and many others might know their unknown-ness.

My parents *believed* that Bob Crumley was buried in the Balgay, or at least my mother did. The truth is as I have explained, and the irony is that the land specifically set aside to honour people just like him was just over the garden wall all that time. I wonder what difference it might have made had they known. I uncovered some evidence to suggest that there had been a bit of a conspir-acy to blacken Bob Crumley's name within his family, and that it may have been imposed on my father's gen-eration by his parents' generation. I wrote a short novel about Bob Crumley, called *The Goalie* (Whittles, 2004), in which I advanced a theory that could explain what happened, but I will never know. What I cannot believe is that my parents deliberately lied about it. Lying was simply not in their nature.

Back down at my parents' grave, I tidied the earth around it as I always do, dead-headed the little rose bush I planted earlier in the year, and thought especially about the man my mother and my brother and I buried forty years before. He was the most practical of men. He left school at fourteen, became a grocer's apprentice, joined

the Army at nineteen (his father's brother, who had con-
nections in London by then, ushered him into the Royal
Horse Artillery, whereas most Dundee men of his generation would have gone into the Black Watch). He com-
pleted ten years in 1939, and was on the reserve list, and
was therefore called up at once when war broke out. He
had an active war. Dunkirk, Normandy, Sicily, North
Africa (Desert Rats, El Alamein, Montgomery's Eighth
Army), and he lived more or less unscathed to tell the tale
and smile for a camera at the Victory Parade in Berlin. He
is leaning on his half-track truck. He was a driver – everything from officer's cars to Jeeps and Scout cars and trucks
of every shape and size and half-tracks. He may have
driven tanks but I don't think so and he never mentioned
them. I have his copy of the Victory Parade programme.

He became a telephone engineer. He loved excellence
in sport, and had represented the Army in athletics, and
passed on his love of football and cricket. One unusual
consequence of his Army life (he went in as a private and
came out in 1945 as a lance-corporal, having declined
promotions) was the enthusiasm with which he watched
show-jumping on television. His uncle's regimental choice
had given him an unlikely love of horses, unlikely at least
for one of his social background, and wherever he travelled in Scotland he would stop the car at a field of horses,
and dispense peppermints to them from a store he kept in
the car specifically for that purpose. I think I saw him feed
horses in almost every county in Scotland.

And he drove a car better than any man I have met
since.

He was an uncomplicated man of simple pleasures. He had no facility for the arts (my mother dished those out to my brother and me in abundance; she was a musician, a painter, a reader, and she insisted that through her mother she – and therefore I – was related to J.M. Barrie, and that was where my love of writing was born. I never checked it out; I prefer to live with the possibility rather than to discover that it was one more ill-conceived family myth). I suppose I hero-worshipped Dad from childhood. He was the kind of father you wanted if you were my kind of child. He was stern when he thought it appropriate, and warm when he wasn't stern. He wanted me to stay on at school and go to university but I wanted out of school sooner rather than later, left at sixteen and became a trainee journalist. I think he may have been disappointed.

One day, late in his life, he was watching me as I tried to carry out some simple domestic chore or other, it might have been changing a plug. I know how to change a plug, but it's not the kind of thing I do with fluency, or interest, for that matter. He watched for a while then he said:

"The trouble is, Jim, you're no good for anything but pushing a pen."

It was the kind of lightweight banter that coursed through our family every day, and it was meant to carry no weight at all, but it did, witness the fact that forty-some-thing years later I still remember. I didn't say anything but I rather took it personally. The thing is, Dad, it turns out you were right. And I still wish you had had the kind of relationship with your father that I had with mine. That I still have with mine.

Chapter Ten

An Audience with
the Great Shepherd

IF THE FIRST OF SEPTEMBER is the first day of Meteorological
Autumn, and if therefore the 31st of November is the last
day, then the 16th of October is midautumn day, the centrepiece of autumn, the fulcrum, when all that is wondrous
about this pivotal time of year alights on ultimate pitch-per-
fect notes of harmony, and for the purposes of this book, a
moment of sublime equipoise. Yet midautumn day, when
you write it like that, looks unfamiliar, even weird, while
midsummer day is not really the middle of anything at all,
but rather the end of something, in this case the Earth's
annual but half-hearted approach towards the sun. We
should do something about that; make Midautumn Day
a national holiday with capital letters, as part of a national
programme to educate the population about the role of the
one truly great season of the year. Until then, it seems to
me that the least I can do is to direct this book's journey
to a truly great landscape, a kind of pilgrimage to the heart
of autumn. A pilgrimage needs a destination, so I chose
the perfect mountain – Buachaille Etive Mòr, the Great
Shepherd of Etive, also known the length and breadth of
the mountaineering world as "The Buachaille", and pro-
nounced "The Boochle". And as luck would have it, I also
chose the perfect day.

⊙ ⊙ ⊙

Traveller, you must always wave to the Rannoch Rowan! If you are unfamiliar with this first commandment of the A82 between the Black Mount and Glencoe, you should know that the Rannoch Rowan stands just yards from the road: you can't miss it, for it grows directly out of a large rock, a glacial erratic carelessly dumped there a few millennia back down the line by a passing glacier. (There are many such rowans scattered across the Highlands that know how to get blood out of a stone, and some are befriended by golden eagles, which carry off sprigs of their leaves to weave with some delicacy into the colossal endeavour of the building and maintenance of their eyries. I have seen them do that every month of the year in which there are rowan leaves to be plucked. It is not clear why they do it, at least it isn't to me, nor why it is thought fit adornment for both the inner and outer walls. And while it is true that they use other greenery too, especially birch leaves, it is surely no coincidence that so many eyries have rock-rooted rowans for neighbours. The very word "greenery" is not always accurate; I have watched an eagle carry a September sprig of bright red rowan leaves to an eyrie, which if it had any use at all so late in the nesting year, it could only have been as a roosting ledge. Golden eagles *like* rowans and perhaps it is as simple as that. So do we: the rowan before the door of Highland houses, both lived-in and ruinous, is as ubiquitous as the rowan at the eagle's door.)

But something in the erect stance of the Rannoch Rowan, its often brutal isolation, and its blatantly conspicuous roadside situation has endeared it to drivers on the A82. And it is the only one I know that has a name. I first came this way as a child on family holidays to the West Highlands in my father's car, and he waved to it. I do not remember exactly how he replied to family questions about the habit, but I think the gist was that it's the Rannoch Rowan and that's what you do. It would not surprise me to learn that the tradition made its way in among the rest of us by way of Scotland's Traveller families. My father certainly knew quite a few of them from his years as a telephone engineer among the backroads of Angus and east Perthshire. But somehow or other, it was impressed into my impression-eager young mind that it was a good thing to do to wave to the Rannoch Rowan each time you passed and to ask for a safe journey. I have done it ever since. Over the years the greeting has contracted to a kind of shorthand. I say: "One more time – safe journey" on the way north, and: "Until the next time – safe journey" on the way back. And I've always had safe journeys.

So in my mind, and for many years now, Glencoe in general and the Buachaille in particular, have begun with the Rannoch Rowan as if it were a herald the mountain gods had sent ahead to announce the imminent presence of the Great Shepherd of Etive, and the particularly rarefied mountain realm of the Coe that lies beyond its mighty, graceful profile. Even if you know what's coming as you top the final crest in the road and the Buachaille begins to rise up out of the land, it is still quite impossible not to succumb to anticipation's thrill. Whatever the weather, what unfolds is Scotland's mountain masterpiece. On that particular Midautumn Day, it was a mountain out of a dream. The sky had slowly emptied of cloud as I drove north and west, and now it was utterly cloudless. The Buachaille looked enthroned in a way that was new to me, one perfect mountain whose very standing in the landscape is so overarchingly dominant *and* beautiful (a phenomenon of worldwide rarity) that only prime autumn adds a daring, zesty, burnt umber frisson to the foreground grasses and even flirts with the hems and pleats of the mountain's skirts, and the sense of nature as a seductress is utterly complete.

My plan was characteristically ill-defined and optimistic. I would park on the Glen Etive road, wander up the River Coupall, find a sunny nook on a bank, and sit at the mountain's feet. Then I would watch it for a while with a notebook and sketchbook, empty my mind, and see what rubbed off. Sometimes, when I don't have a better idea, that's what I do.

The name puzzles me. Why "Shepherd"? And why is the same name afforded to its next-door neighbour, Buachaille Etive Beag, the lower hill simply being named as the diminutive of the Great Shepherd? If, as seems likely, they were named from settlements at the head of Loch Etive, where the two mountains appear cheek-by-jowl, there is nothing shepherd-like about their appearance. Perhaps they were named from a time when the people placed their notion of a god on mountaintops, and they had already imbued that god with the notion of a guardian of the flock, which was later attributed to Christianity. Or maybe something fundamental was lost in translation over the millennia. I'm going with that as the most likely explanation. And anyway, the first thing that struck me when I found my sunny nook on the banks of the Coupall was that the Buachaille, from that vantage point, is the most feminine of mountains, a Great Shepherdess. There again, back in the days of the namers-of-the-landscape, perhaps their language made no distinction between "shepherd" and "shepherdess".

I began by just sitting and looking. I am an admirer of this of all mountains. I have climbed it four or five times and circumnavigated it once. With the help of a former newspaper colleague I climbed it by way of Curved Ridge, the beginning and end of my rock-climbing career. It is rock-climbing for beginners, but a sensational way to climb the mountain, for it leans close to the Rannoch Wall (famed rock-climbing theatre) and it unlocked for me something of a sense of the inner mountain, something of the workings of nature as sculptor that created such a work of art of the highest order. It is such an individualist, such a landmark of such raw, incomparable beauty, and it is in moments like this that I find fault with the Munro-bagging fad that has shaped modern Scottish mountaineering. I have trouble with the idea of Buachaille Etive Mòr as something collectable to be ticked off and lumped in with every other mountain in the land because it happens to qualify on the grounds of a spurious height limit. To climb such a mountain, just to "collect" it, is not a good enough reason.

Then I remembered that I had sat right here years ago now, sifting my way through a similar train of thought, and that I had written down the result in an old book, long out of print, called *Glencoe – Monarch of Glens* (Baxter, 1990). I had considered the Buachaille's work-of-art status then too, had mischievously re-categorised it, not a Munro but a MacDiarmid of a mountain, and had quoted the great poet in support of my argument:

> *...and the principal question*
> *Aboot a work o' art is frae hoo deep*
> *A life it springs – and syne hoo faur*
> *Up frae't it has the poo'er to leap.*

And then I summoned my favourite painter to my cause:

> *Paul Cézanne said: "What art is primarily about is what the eye thinks." His eye thought so much of one mountain, Mont St Victoire at Aix-en-Provence, he thought it worth painting again and again for ever, the mountain growing in stature and abstraction the more he painted it, the more his eye thought about it. My eye thinks much the same when I sit under Buachaille Etive Mòr, studious and seduced. It is a mountain to satisfy a Cézanne. Circumnavigate the Buachaille, shape and re-shape it, build and re-build all its landforms, let your eye paint its every profile again and again forever until it is a familiarity you crave, until you must breathe the Buachaille, not air. Know then what love impelled Cézanne, intimately alone with his mountain, what Buachailles we'd have seen if only Glencoe had a climate like Aix-en-Provence...*

Now, the better part of thirty years later, and without consciously making that old association, I was reaching out to the same mountain as the symbolic embodiment of autumn. The simplicity of its shape from the banks of the

Coupall is central to the notion, an almost perfect isosceles triangle, such a shape as children would reach for if you asked them to draw a mountain. The shape is a deception, of course, because what you see from here is only the Rannoch-inclined east face of Buachaille Etive Mòr, beyond which (and out of sight) a long ridge runs westward, a heady highway slung through the airspace that binds Glen Etive and Glencoe. But the pyramidal aspect is so persuasive that it perfectly represented what I had envisaged when I considered the possibilities of a destination for this book. I saw it as a meandering journey to a particular time and place that turned out to be this time and this place, not just the summit of this particular land but the summit, the highest endeavour, of autumn itself. From here and now, the book's journey will lead back again by way of lesser summits and foothills to the land of the Highland Edge where it began. I have always enjoyed descents more than ascents, and from this zenith of the endeavour, the sense of what still lay ahead between Midautumn Day and the last day of November excited me. I sat warming myself in early afternoon sun, watching a blue-black swathe of deepest shadow creep round the mountain as the sun westered.

I shifted my focus to more immediate surroundings for a while, which is the kind of diversity that a long stillness encourages. In the right circumstances it can lead your eye from the golden eagle crossing distant watersheds to the wren at your feet, or from an island-strewn ocean to a clutch of plover eggs in a nest of stones. Under the Buachaille, I shifted my gaze from the mountain and started to explore the grasses themselves, this high watermark of that moorland-sea called Rannoch, an image which is greatly strengthened just by turning to look behind, to where the land opens out into Scotland's most spectacular land-locked space, at the far edge of which it is possible to make out the tiny blue shape of Schiehallion. The sheer scope of the space is what assists the notion of a moorland sea.

The grass was enlivened everywhere by the fading, withering stalks and leaves and heads of wild flowers that a month before still brushed the land with their own hot and cool shades of sparks and flames. Finally I reached for notebook and pen, made quick and ill-considered reference sketches, then out of one more thoughtless stillness came patterns of words.

Buachaille (Shepherd)

At my feet the flotsam
of the moor: the bog triptych
– cotton, myrtle, asphodel –
and bluebell, sundew, tormentil,
mountain grass, heather, lichen, moss,
finished fragrance of orchids.

And glaring down from within
the upgathered robes of Etive
the Shepherd saw my pencil hand
measure a sundew with a thumbnail,
then raise the same thumb
at arm's length to measure
the whole Shepherd from robe-hem
to mountainous pow.

And in the evening the Shepherd
enfolded all that grew there,
and the quiet deer, golden eagle,
raven, owl, lost wolf howl;
but I remained unfolded, beyond
the Shepherd's reach. I must
go on or coldly wait the dawn.

Have you ever simply sat and watched a mountain over, say, three hours, long enough to observe the evolving action of sunlight and shadow, and to realise how these alone affect your own sense of the nature of the mountain? Drive past the mountain, or pause just long enough to take its photograph and drive on again, and your souvenir is nothing but a moment in the mountain's life. Climb it and you are too close to achieve a sense of the whole mountain as it eases through a succession of moods. But sit – just sit – and make no gesture towards it beyond your complete engagement with it so that you begin to fathom in your long stillness what it might take to be a rock. I have written elsewhere about how I once sat and watched a perched golden eagle for four hours, during which it did nothing at all beyond scratching its bill with a claw and look around the sky; and how I recognised my limitations then in the matter of sitting and watching eagles sitting and watching and doing nothing, and how it was still there when I left and it might have been there all night and I wish I knew. But one of the things it taught me was an awareness of my own limitations in nature's company, how nature can out-distance me and out-wait me at more or less every turn. It is as well to learn to accept that state of affairs because acceptance brings with it the knowledge that nature's needs are best satisfied when they do not have to share a landscape with people. No matter how well-intentioned our presence may be, it is a fact that nature is better off when our backs are turned. But none of that should stop you from sitting quietly and alone from time to time in the company of a beautiful mountain or a tree or quiet sea flowing between, say, a Mull clifftop and Staffa.

The sky above the Buachaille had emptied of cloud hours ago, and the utter blueness was at its deepest directly above the summit, and that shade seemed to seep into the very buttresses on its sun-smitten flank, and into the shadow that edged towards the middle of the mountain as the afternoon dwindled down. The foreground was the river, whisky shaded, its midstream rocks pale grey and fawn. The far bank was embellished by the deep bronze of withering bracken. Beyond and between the fronds, blue-black banks of peat in deep shadow were topped by friezes of vividly lit heather, blaeberries and bog myrtle bushes. The tallest, wispiest grasses were pale pink, and these shimmered above tussocks of citrus shades – orange, lemon and lime green, and all these harmonised into distance and relentlessly rising eddies of that burnt-umber cloak that fed the lowest reaches of the mountain. Finally, a single tiny white cloud appeared and came and stood by the summit for a few minutes, during which it slowly dematerialised before my eyes. I photographed it, and somehow even that least intrusive of actions damaged the palpable magic, the mystery of what persuades a cloud to form alone in an empty sky, to drift as if by design to this of all mountaintops, and then vanish as if it had never been. The photograph shows it had been, of course, but it doesn't tell me anything I didn't know.

Then, far over my shoulder, a red deer stag roared, and changed the nature of the moment, the hour, the afternoon, the day.

⊙ ⊙ ⊙

The red deer rut often bursts into full-throated, anthemic pageant with the first frost. But September and early October had produced barely a whiff of frost, and I had encountered nothing but half-hearted overtures on my travels. But this sounded more authentic. I had spent the better part of four hours in the mountain's company, and now what promised to be a memorably lingering late afternoon and early evening (the light was already yellowing delightfully) turned my thoughts towards the deer, and how – and where – I might make the most of such a golden opportunity. I like woodland and red deer together, and so, for that matter, do red deer, for they are – they *should* be – woodland animals. They prosper in woodland. What stops them from being woodlanders over much of Highland Scotland is the human perversion of nature's scheme of things known as the Highland deer forest, in which the only thing that grows branches is a set of antlers. Centuries of treating both the red deer and the red grouse (the grouse moor is the equivalent perversion of the deer forest) as economic sacred cows, and manipulating the land and all the wild creatures that live there (not to mention the ones that should and could still live there, which the "sporting estate" mentality has rendered extinct) have impoverished the natural landscape to such an extent that the expression "wet desert" becomes ever more appropriate. Absence of anything like natural predators means that red deer are routinely fenced out of new woodland projects, and one way or another they have been banished to the open hill, and there they suffer a most unnatural way of life.

But I had in mind a theatre of the red deer rut where at least the illusion of some interaction between deer and woodland is intact. It is also perfectly placed for the reintroduction of those missing species that would make a truly significant, benevolent impact on the biodiversity of wild Scotland, notably beaver and wolf. The stag voices that now began to reach me from both Rannoch Moor and Glen Etive put the place in mind. I packed up, I said my farewells to the mountain, and headed back down the main road to Bridge of Orchy, thence on the single track towards Inveroran and the woodland-and-loch-and-mountain sorcery of Doire Darach.

It is a strange name. *Doire* is Gaelic for an oak copse; *darach* is an oak tree. But Doire Darach is an ancient pinewood remnant with a few larch and a lot of birch. Just to the south-west is another pinewood remnant at Glen Fuar and just to the north-east yet another at Crannach, all the proof anyone needs that Scots-pine-dominated forest cover was once nature's preferred option hereabouts. The particular attraction of Doire Darach is that it stands on the shore of Loch Tulla and the lovely wetland flourish at its west end, and it looks out beyond the loch to the mighty ridge-and-corrie mountain showpiece that is Stob Ghabhar. A few decades ago now, Doire Darach's owner was something of a pioneer in pinewood restoration using small, fenced plots to expand and enhance the surviving woodland. The results so impressed the Nature Conservancy Council that it adopted a policy of encouraging further restoration projects.

I slipped inside the inevitable deer fence and the first thing I saw was what looked like the disembodied head of a red deer staggie lying in the grass beyond an inlet of the loch. It confirmed that it was not disembodied by twitching awkwardly at my arrival, then twitching the other way when an unseen stag roared from the trees. So was it stuck in the mud? Or was it just dying? Or was it comfortably resting on a warm and sunlit couch of firm ground that I couldn't see? I tended towards the idea that it was in some kind of trouble, but without a boat there was no way for me to get anywhere near it. I found a dry pine root to sit on, to watch it for a while, and to let the drama of the red deer rut unfold as evening began to ease in across the landscape, scattering shadows and low-slung beams of yellow light. There was a beautiful twisted spray of yellow bracken beside my pine tree, and all the blueberries I could eat. For the second time in a single day dedicated to some sense of autumn's high water mark, I found myself becalmed by a kind of idyll. Nature was gilding its own lily, and the effect was bewitching. My favourite lines of Seton Gordon crept into my mind. They are from *The Cairngorm Hills of Scotland* (Cassell, 1925):

In the immense silences of these wild corries and dark rocks,
the spirit of the high and lonely places revealed herself, so that
one felt the serene and benign influence that has from time to
time caused men to leave the society of their fellows and live
on some remote and sun-drenched isle – as St Cuthbert did on
Farne – there to steep themselves in those spiritual influences
that are hard to receive in the crowded hours of human life.

My book about the return of Scotland's beavers, *Nature's Architect* (Saraband, 2015), had been published earlier in the year, and I was constantly reappraising the landscapes of Scotland with beaver potential in mind. I thought how perfect this end of Loch Tulla would be. That book's predecessor, *The Eagle's Way*, had alighted on this very shore with sea eagles in mind, for a tiny rocky islet in the loch with a couple of defiant trees was identified by John Love as a historic sea eagle nest site. Love had spearheaded the very first sea eagle reintroduction project on Rum in the 1970s and he had trawled the country for evidence of known sea eagle nesting sites. And Seton Gordon, who died aged ninety just three years after Love's project had begun, wrote of another sea eagle nest on a birch tree on an island in Loch Ba, about five miles away. Ospreys have already returned to Loch Tulla, and given that suitable conditions for ospreys are often suitable for sea eagles too, and given the young sea eagle's tendency for wandering among its historic heartlands, it is only a matter of time before it nests around these waters again.

By the autumn of 2015, beavers from the unofficial Tayside population had already reached the far side of

Rannoch Moor under their own steam, and beavers from the official trial release in Knapdale were within easy reach of Loch Tulla. Here is where they will meet someday soon. And this vast landscape both behind and ahead of me, from the Black Wood of Rannoch to the shores of Loch Etive and Loch Awe, and with Doire Darach and Loch Tulla as a kind of lynchpin where east meets west, is one of limitless potential for innovative nature conservation on the grand scale. From the re-foresting of Rannoch Moor to the reintroduction of Scotland's wolves (their demise was 200 years later than that of Scotland's beavers), thereby implementing nature's ancient method of controlling deer populations and enabling the co-existence of native woodland and native red deer herds, and to the beaver-fuelled expansion and restoration of Scotland's desperately depleted wetlands… all that can be achieved right here, and can serve as a showpiece for enlightened nature conservation for landowners to copy and the rest of the world to admire.

An hour drifted past, the light evolved from lemon shades to deep gold. The rut began to give voice, and to intensify. I became aware of at least six stags calling from six different compass points, although as yet I could see none of them. The nearest voice was in the woods across the loch. I stared through the binoculars at those trees and once caught up with a moving shadow that must surely have been a deer, but looked like nothing more than a mobile piece of woodland. Slowly, the realisation grew that the voices were all closing in on the loch. I looked for the staggie's head, and found it in exactly the same place, still turning from time to time to follow the stags' conversation of challenge and counter-challenge. Suddenly a ten-pointer with a grey muzzle and neck appeared splashing across the river to the west of the loch and climbing its far bank onto a level patch of turf, and less than 200 yards away. There he stopped and stared along his back, and in that pose, unleashed an unearthly roar, which was matched at once by an unseen beast in the trees, unseen but closing. These, I guessed, were the voices of vanquished and the victor in that order.

There was an immediate and astonishing consequence. The staggie with the disembodied head suddenly sprang effortlessly to his feet and edged away from the old bruiser beyond the river. I thought I might call him Lazarus.

The evening began to drowse, the hearing was becoming easier but picking out the individual stags was almost impossible, and I had an eighty-miles drive ahead of me. I drove south with a headful of shapely mountains rising from a lightly woven blanket of native forest, of roaring stags, of beaver muzzles furrowing a still, pale watersheet and, from the edge of the highest pines, the woodwind discords of wolfsong. If you cannot dream such dreams in such a landscape on such a Midautumn Day, you shouldn't be allowed to dream.

◎ ◎ ◎

A few days later I watched a television programme that featured a deer farm, and showed staff sawing off the antlers of red deer stags so that "the animals don't get hurt".

Chapter Eleven

Swan Songs

SWAN SONG – it is an odd expression, generally credited to Shakespeare: "I will play the song and die in music", said Emilio in *Othello*. But Shakespeare was no one's idea of a naturalist, and the most likely explanation of that line is that he was familiar with an already established scrap of folklore and simply gave it a voice. Yet the idea endures and has gone into the language: a swan song is a final endeavour. But there is no biological evidence to support the idea that a swan's dying gesture is a song. On the other had, the song of swans is my idea of autumn's soundtrack, for the arrival of the whooper swans on migration from Iceland or Scandinavia is a brassy blast of an ancient heraldry from the edge of the Arctic Circle that puts chills of anticipation between my shoulder blades. If I am honest, no other bird has quite the hold on me that the whooper swan does. The whole tribe of swans, from ubiquitous mutes to Australian blacks and North American trumpeters, has captivated me for many years, but something in the sound and the sight of a skein of whoopers in flight adds a presence, an Arctic edge, to a Scottish autumn that somehow embodies my fascination for the northern places of the earth. There is a Celtic or Norse (or both!) legend that the souls of princes fly on after death in the form of whooper swans. Flying from Iceland to Scotland every autumn, and back again every spring, is my idea of what immortality might look like.

The autumn of 1989 was an extraordinary one for people of my persuasion, extraordinary for an event that is as indelible in my mind today as it was on the day I drove 200 miles to witness it. I left Stirling at dawn on the long haul up the A9 to the edge of the Cairngorms. I noticed that the Insh Marshes, one of my favourite places on Earth and one of the most reliable of autumn and winter whooper swan haunts, was empty. That fitted with what I had heard. The mountains were snow and gold. The roads were all but empty. October Tuesdays are quiet in the eastern Highlands. Just past Aviemore I counted my 20th buzzard of the journey. I paused for coffee and the view of new snow on the mountains around the Lairig Ghru, and I wished briefly that I was going there, but my destination was two hours further north. I skirted Inverness, crossed the Kessock Bridge, and drove on, a willing slave, for the moment, to the A9. Halfway between the Cromarty Firth and the Dornoch Firth I finally turned off into a quiet landscape of low hills and woods and hard-won farms. Almost at once a male hen harrier lifted slow and gull-coloured from a roadside fence, not from a post but from the top wire of the fence itself, which looked precarious to my non-harrier eyes, but I imagine it knew what it was doing when it preferred wire to post. Then the sky filled up with clouds and clouds of geese. I had reached Loch Eye.

Whooper swans had been making headlines here, even in the kind of newspapers that could not be relied upon to tell the difference between a swan and a turkey. Raw spectacle had turned the nation's head. Something like half of all the whooper swans that could be expected to migrate from Iceland to Scotland in the whole of autumn had turned up in a couple of days and stayed. And I had just driven 200 miles to see what 2,000 swans looked like on a loch three miles long by a mile wide. Not knowing what to expect, I parked a discreet distance from the loch and while it was still out of sight. As soon as I stepped from the car, the sound was unlike anything that had ever assailed my ears before. It was not so much loud as impenetrable, thick, a thing of layered depths, so that no individual voice was discernible. If someone had told me that it was the sound of a great army on the march in the distance, I could have been persuaded. I walked through woods to a boggy shore, parted a few last leaves and looked out on the loch for the first time. I had expected a watersheet smothered in whooper swans. What I had not expected was just as many mute swans, several times as many geese, and (to me at least) uncountable hordes of duck, which, I would learn later, included 50,000 wigeon.

Loch Eye is well known as a wildfowl destination and a staging post for Icelandic whoopers on the way south. The sheer weight of numbers in October 1989 was apparently the result of a particularly vigorous growth of a pondweed called ruppia, a bounty that far exceeded the norm. But how did the swans know it was there? What sophisticated secret code of communication reached from the Black Isle to Iceland? Whooper migration to Scotland begins around mid-September, peaks in mid-to-late October and dwindles down towards the end of November, and some will head for the Hebrides and the west coast route to more southerly wintering grounds and some will head for the east coast or a middle route down through the heart of the country. But that autumn, 2,000 swans left en masse for a single destination because there was an ample food supply to sustain a feeding frenzy. What manner of intelligence made that possible?

Loch Eye became a city of swans. In every direction and as far as I could see across the water, swans fed and loafed and preened and bickered and blethered and took off and landed and dozed and woke and startled and calmed down again. And all of this was conducted to that insistent, unrelenting thrum of bird voices: every shade of whooper brassiness, every snort and grunt and soft shriek of the mute swan's often surprising repertoire, ear-splitting wigeon whistles seared through the mass like rockets, dozens at a time, while the goose hordes rumbled in rising and falling dense clouds off and on the surface of the water, and marauding mobs of waders cruised between the shallows and the nearest fields. Occasionally it was possible to pin down one alarm or another to the hopeful presence of a passing hen harrier or a peregrine or a sparrowhawk in search of the inevitable casualties and invalids that must make up a small percentage of such a press of wildfowl.

Swans in flight are simply among the most aesthetically striking gestures of nature at work, and as a rule I can never get enough of them. Wherever I encounter them they stop me in my tracks. But this was swan flight of a different order, swan flight on a scale of mathematical improbability. They flew in short sorties across the water a few hundred yards at a time. They flew in angry charges that barely left the water. They flew in wide circuits of the loch. They flew in from the fields and out to the fields. They flew in tight arrowheads or three at a time, or in pairs, or alone. They flew in long, low skeins of ten or twenty or fifty, forging an unswerving route above the heads of the swimming masses, more reminiscent of sea-going gannets. They banked before shoreline trees or heaved up over them at the last moment (I saw only one misjudgement that ended in an unwieldy slaister of thrashing wings and tumbling twigs and branches, but I imagine it must have happened dozens of times a day). Away and away across the water, swans flew in every direction and for every conceivable and inconceivable purpose. To latch on to one particular flightpath in the glasses was to cross ten, twenty, fifty others in contrary directions at any one moment. Focal points were as elusive as thistledown. Everything was a focal point but only for as long as I could resist the contrary pull of every other distraction that filled the glasses.

Eventually I gave up on the glasses and just settled to watch and let the whole symphonic wonder of the thing wash over me. I stayed half a day. Dusk brought no let-up in activity, no quietening of the massed voices, no lessening of the spectacle other than that it softened around the edges a little. A buzzard crossed my shore, high and crying, and circled three times. How I envied that bird at that moment. To be able to soar to a few hundred feet above the water and linger there, looking down – that would be something.

I walked back to the car, stowed my pack and changed from wellies to shoes then slipped into the driving seat and closed the door and the silence hit me like a physical force. Yes, there is a swansong, it is the wild music of 5,000 swan throats making wondrous symphonic mayhem, and it celebrates not death but life, swans' life and my own life for the way it has been enriched by swans.

◉ ◉ ◉

Loch Leven is a large, shallow Lowland water where Fife and Kinross rub shoulders, a National Nature Reserve with the RSPB wetland reserve of Vane Farm on its south shore, and an easy half-hour drive from where I live. In the late October of 2015, I found it happed in a cold, grey pallor, the water dead-still. The footpath that encircles the entire loch offers unlimited scope for birdwatching, with formal seats and picnic spots, or you can go off-piste among shore-line woods and reed beds for a more furtive experience. I enjoy both options, but on such a quiet day I am more than happy with a wooden bench, an al fresco lunch, a wide view over almost the entire ten square miles of the loch, and a loose scattering of around 150 whooper swans close in to the shore around the loch's south-east corner. Further out were healthy numbers of mutes, geese, mergansers, goosanders, pochard, goldeneye and tufted ducks. Any long autumn-in-to-winter vigil on this water is likely to be invigorated by the drop-in presence of a sea eagle. As the east coast reintroduction on the Tay estuary begins to consolidate and bear fruit, Loch Leven has become a regular feature of their far-travelled explorations, and while I have never seen one tackle a swan

I have heard of one mid-air attempt not too far from here, and they can certainly take on a goose, although with the huge numbers of duck and waders at Loch Leven it's hard to imagine they would bother. There again, logic is not always the determining factor when a sea eagle selects a target.

I listened as much as I watched, for unlike Loch Eye all those years ago, and despite the clearly audible voices of a large congregation of swans a mile up the loch, I was enjoying the constant chatter among the few dozen birds just offshore and no more than a hundred yards away from where I was sitting. Unlike mute swans, whoopers can turn up the volume when it suits them (it is not always clear *why* it suits them). When they do, they often sustain it for a few minutes at a time and it often involves pairs of birds, and sometimes several pairs. They deal in discords, in a way that makes me think of wolves howling. Harmony is accidental, and as soon as it occurs they slip out of it.

Whooper swans are the most Ellingtonian of brass and reed players, working mostly within a range of a single octave and pitched tonally within the middle register of a flugelhorn or the lower register of a soprano sax. Within that, the phrases are mostly arrangements of pairs of semi-quavers and triplets, thirds and minor thirds, ascending or descending, with occasional variations into fourths and augmented fifths.

And this was exactly the kind of visually uninspiring day that lent itself to a listening ear, and if like mine, the listening ear has had a decades-long schooling in the wiles of jazz, then there are rich pickings. For example, I had begun to notice that within this group of birds, every once in a while, a single voice would explore possibilities out-with the normal octave and at both ends of it. There was a decidedly *whoo-oo* flourish – like a tawny owl on steroids, high-pitched and double fortissimo – from a bird screened by shoreline shrubs, and so startling that I scrambled down to the shore to see if I could identify the caller, but there was a family group of seven there, and they drifted off at my sudden appearance, exchanging quiet *whoop!* monosyllables from within the mainstream range. I headed back up to my comfortable berth and, with my back turned, the same call resounded again. I stopped, turned, considered going back to the shore, smiled to myself and went back to my lunch. Late in the afternoon, having walked a mile or so along the east shore I came across another group of whoopers, both adults and five of that year's youngsters, a healthy brood. From their midst there emerged a baritone-sax-like note that emerged into the still air in the unflattering tonal zone of a fart. For as long as I have been accustomed to keeping their company, whooper swans have made me smile.

The cloud lowered towards the end of the afternoon, a few snowflakes fell, the air grew chilly, and the light had acquired an almost limitless palette of layered greys. A landscape painter friend of mine insists that grey is her favourite colour. Retracing my steps round the shore through a profound quiet, in which my own footfall and the occasional muted brass of the swans were the only sounds, and feeling very much like a mobile fragment of that many-greyed landscape, the hour felt almost sacred, and I had a glimpse into a world that made me understand where she was coming from.

Chapter Twelve

Three Rivers

1: The Tay, Dunkeld

I LOVE REDWOODS, that tribe of arboreal giants that inhabits the west coast of America, but which, in ones and twos and occasional small groves, graces landscapes and gardens over much of Britain. Their towering presence is among the reasons that part of Perthshire likes to preen itself in the words of an Americanism aimed squarely at the tourist trade – Big Tree Country. The Tay at Dunkeld is a favourite haunt of mine at any season of the year, but none better than this one. I decided to make its redwoods the centrepiece of an autumn expedition, but I was unexpectedly waylaid by a dead fish. Sometimes a nature writer's day works out that way.

The Tay just upstream from Dunkeld is a colourful water. Whatever the season, it is filled with solid blocks of colour, reflected abstractions of the trees that line both banks, and on these the current works a particularly subtle sorcery, bending the shapes into wavering curves, and into what I would imagine is a landscape painter's delight. But for a mere nature writer who becomes tongue-tied and ham-fisted with a brush in his hand, why worry about achieving a particular hypnotic effect with a brush when nature has already done it for you and all you have to do is write it down?

Some fluke of the current by the far bank at the Mouse Trap (the salmon pools hereabouts have been named with a particularly quirky charm) was drifting an old cache of washed out, tea-stained oak leaves *upstream*, like a beaver pushing a branch in its jaws, until it slowed to a standstill, caught the edge of an underwater swirl that tugged it inevitably into the mainstream, and it suddenly headed off at a leisurely lope for Dunkeld, for Perth, for all I know. But about the dead fish...

At the base of the far bank, a brain-verses-brawn battle was underway. Brawn appeared to have the upper hand. A piece of fish, much disfigured and mutilated and missing both ends, lay a few inches above the water level on a flat shelf between two small rocks where (I am guessing) it had been abandoned by an otter. A juvenile herring gull was in possession, but it had two ravens for company and these were watching and awaiting opportunity with the patience of the river itself. They stood a few inches beyond the lunging range of the gull's troublesome bill. The gull had been feeding well for some time, but any one raven has more brains than any five herring gulls put together, and here there were two ravens, so the odds were that, once they put their mind to a plan, the gull was on a hiding to nothing. They duly put their minds to a plan.

One of them moved towards the gull's tail in a series of small, sideways hops, a few furtive steps at a time, carefully out of range. The gull was disconcerted, curved its body towards its tail and snapped at the raven. In the two seconds that manoeuvre occupied, the first raven darted in, speared a mouthful of fish and jumped backwards. Now the gull was annoyed, rattled, distressed and no longer in control of the situation. It was about to eat again when the second raven grabbed its tail, gave it a tweak, let go and jumped backwards in rather less time than it takes to tell. The gull screeched and spun round in its own length, but the tail-tweaker had seen that coming and was suddenly three feet off the ground. The gull snapped on thin air, and at the crucial moment the first raven grabbed another sizeable chunk of fish.

It was too much. The gull grabbed the entire fish – or what was left of it – and attempted to fly with it. It flew alright, but the fish broke in two and the larger piece by far was still on the rock, and there were two ravens standing on it and kronking their triumph, and marching round it with an unashamedly gloating strut. The gull retreated, guzzled its mouthful in a single convulsion and accepted defeat. In nature as in democracy, sometimes the other guy wins and that's just the way it is.

◉ ◉ ◉

So that was the diversion that had stalled my expedition to see the redwoods. They are, of course, Californian, the context in which somehow the phrase Big Tree Country sounds more at home. To be sure, Perthshire has big trees, but the redwoods of California are altogether – what's the word I'm looking for? – BIGGER. And in California, another name for the giant sequoia is Bigtree, and they spell it like that with a capital letter, and they live in Bigtree Country.

There are two species of redwoods, the coast redwood (*Sequoia sempervirens*), and, on the western slopes of the Sierra Nevada, the giant sequoia (*Sequoiadendron giganteum*). The coast trees reach up to 350 feet, the giant sequoia to a meagre 280 feet, but as the size of all trees is measured by their mass rather than their height, the giant sequoias are officially the world's biggest trees, hence Bigtrees.

John Muir, inevitably, had something memorable to say about them. In *The Mountains of California* (1894), he wrote:

> *The majestic sequoia is here, too, the king of conifers, the noblest of all the noble race. These colossal trees are as wonderful in fineness of beauty and proportion as in stature – an assemblage of conifers surpassing all that have ever yet been discovered in the forests of the world.*

Or, for that matter, the forests of Perthshire.

Donald Culross Peattie, another fine American nature writer who would develop Muir's theme a century later, described the giant sequoia as "king" of the plants and "the oldest and mightiest of living things". (He might get an argument about age from the Fortingall Yew, but mighty – or big – it is not!) In his book *A Natural History of Western Trees* (Houghton Mifflin, 1953), he went on to characterise the coast redwood as "a queen among trees, a fit mate for the craggier, grandeur of the Bigtree of the Sierra Nevada".

And if your reference point for these tree species is, say, the Tay at Dunkeld or the Royal Botanic Gardens in

Edinburgh, then Peattie is about to knock your socks off, as they say in California:

Constituting all that is left of the once widespread genus, Sequoia, these two species salute each other from widely separated mountain systems. The Redwood inhabit the north Coast Ranges where they are maintained in a coolhouse atmosphere by long baths in sea fogs, unviolated by storms. In contrast, the home of the Giant Sequoia, lying between 6,000 and 8,000 feet altitude on the western slopes of the Sierra is Olympian... The winters have an annual snowfall of ten to twelve feet, but drifts may pile up among the titans thirty feet deep – a mere white anklet to such trees.

And Ralph Waldo Emerson, maybe the greatest of all American tree watchers, added this hymn of praise in his essay *Nature* (James Munroe, 1836):

Within these plantations of God, a decorum and sanctity reign, a perennial festival is dressed, and the guest sees not how he should tire of them in a thousand years. In the woods, we return to reason and faith.

And amen to that noblest of final thoughts.

At Dunkeld, you encounter two giants, giants by the standards of Perthshire, and you rather stumble on them because they grow in the midst of a woodland of lesser trees that screen their presence until you find them, each in its own small clearing (in this kind of company they rather insist on that) among oaks, beeches, hollies, chestnuts… and they are rooted within yards of each other and at the same elevation. Oh, but even one at a time they brook astonishment, and your mind reels at the girth of the trunks, at the sheer reach of them before they display anything like a branch. The bark is six inches thick and I find myself wondering if the treecreepers that nest and roost here *inside* the bark appreciate the difference between the possibilities of redwoods compared to, say, a Scots pine. Excavating a roost was never easier, but what do they make of their corkscrewing progress up such a tree that just goes on and on and on and up and up and up?

And when they do eventually encounter a branch, it is unlikely to be an ordinary kind of branch. An American scientist recorded that, on the biggest of all the Bigtrees, the first branch he encountered was 150 feet above the ground. But it was six feet in diameter and 150 feet long, and it was held horizontally by the incomprehensible strength of its parent tree. Think about it. And if you are a treecreeper, the world as you know it has just been redefined. If you have a redwood near you (there is even a helpful website, www.redwoodworld.co.uk), and you are accustomed to pause and marvel as you pass, it is good to know that on the west coast of America they stand in their thousands, often so close together that a man cannot pass between them. Transatlantic travel is an unspeakable ordeal in my book, and I have put up with it only once because the destination was Alaska and the BBC Natural History Unit was paying. If there was one other destination that might just lure me back, it would be to see the redwood forests, "the noblest of all the noble race". For the time being, then, I wandered out along the banks of the Tay from Dunkeld, pausing to watch a tussle over a dead fish or a vigorous salmon thrashing the waters of the Girnal, agreeable distractions both on my small pilgrimage to see the redwoods of Big Tree Country, and thereby to afford the imagination a knowing glimpse of their transatlantic kin that stand up to their ankles in thirty feet of snow.

2: The Earn, near Comrie

Much of the fieldwork for my beaver book, *Nature's Architect*, was carried out on the River Earn near Comrie in heartland Perthshire, but it was not there that I first discovered first-hand evidence of just how far the outer limits of the "accidental" Tayside beaver population had reached. That was on a little backwater of the Leny just outside Callander, a small beaver dam that created a stretch of calm water out of reach of the mainstream. I am as sure as I can be that it was the work of a single beaver that did not linger long. But two years later, and not withstanding some spectacular winter floods in the area, the dam was still there, broken and sagging admittedly, and if you had never seen it when it was intact you might not give it a second glance now. But from time to time I wander that way just to see if there has been any further beaver incursion into what would be perfect habitat.

In mid-October, 2015, I made yet another visit, for the site is right in the heart of what I think of as my writer's territory and less than a half-hour drive from home. The discovery I made that day was not the one I had been hoping for these past two years, but rather the first small sign of the landscape evolution that kicks in once beavers have moved on: the top of the dam was thick with leaves. Wherever people have lived with and studied beavers for many years, they emphasise the benevolent evolution that emanates directly from their architecture and from their impact on woodland and wetland. My American friend, David Carroll, a New Hampshire-based nature writer and wildlife artist of distinction, and a wetland specialist, is one such person. In *Nature's Architect* I quoted from his captivating book, *Swampwalker's Journal – A Wetland Year* (Houghton Mifflin, 1999):

> *I follow a stream course to a series of long-abandoned beaver ponds. The dams that created these impoundments have been eroded over time by water and ice and by what Robert Frost termed "the slow, smokeless burning of decay". Deep-muck sediments collect in the lingering ruins of the beavers' work, and here wetland gardens grow. The afternoon air is scented by the leaves of wild mint I crush in traversing the bottom pilings of a dam. Spring-blue and brightly golden-eyed, uncoiling wands of forget-me-not, another plant that finds a niche on woodland beaver dams, edge the green mint in clusters. Beaver dams that have fallen into desuetude become profuse botanical gardens of wetland plants not adapted to flooded ponds or the saturated muck of drained ones.*

A small symptom of that process is what I had just discovered on my Callander backwater. It prompted me to go back to the Earn, and to see what had happened in my absence since *Nature's Architect* was published. There is a danger for a generalist nature writer like me that I become focussed on a particular species for the time it takes to research and write and promote a new book, then neglect the continuing possibilities of the theme under the weight of the demands of the next project. The dangers of that particular pitfall are mitigated, at least, by the fact that over the last decade I have been working on a sequence of books dealing with nature's big themes (whales, wolves, native woodland, eagles, beavers) and that none of these can be treated in isolation from all the others. To study one is to discover new perspectives on the others. It matters to me that I expand my knowledge base so that I always keep nature's bigger picture in the back of my mind. The beavers' story did not stop writing itself the day I finished my book. So with the "slow, smokeless burning of decay" in my mind I headed back to the Earn.

I began by checking on a group of trees the beavers had felled to bridge an inlet of the river that flowed between the bank and a small islet of mud. Both the inlet and the islet were the beavers' doing. The felled trees, I had begun to speculate, were a prelude to the establishment of a new lodge, the entrance to which would lead directly from the quietened water of the inlet. One tree still stood. It was the first beaver-gnawed tree I ever found, about two years before. For months afterwards, the beavers would return to it and bite out another few inches of trunk, then leave it again. The bright white of the gnawed wood and the piles of woodchips at the base of the trunk were measurable evidence of the latest assault on the tree. Over time, the exposed wood darkened to brown. Now, it was grey. No beaver had been anywhere near it for quite a while. The only thing that changed was that, where the felled trees lay on the islet, they had now acquired the company of a piece of the wooden walkway that had been laid on a fisherman's path across a bog. It was about fifteen feet long, eighteen inches wide and two inches thick, and my best guess was that it had been manoeuvred onto the islet by beavers when the river was high. This seemed to strengthen the notion that a new dam or a lodge was planned for the quiet water of the inlet. But that apart, there was no new sign of beaver life at all.

Perhaps they had moved on, although it was not immediately clear to my non-beaver eyes and instincts that they had eaten themselves out of habitat. But a little further upstream, where they had built a canal about fifty yards long and begun to dam and deepen a pool at the downstream end, the canal was dry and the pool only inches deep where it had been several feet deep. And there was no sign of new tree-felling activity there either.

The other possibility was the one I am less than eager to contemplate, but elsewhere in Perthshire and in Angus, farmers and estate managers had responded to beaver works on their land by destroying the dams and lodges and shooting the beavers. Incredibly, this state of affairs was entirely legal despite the fact that a report of the findings of the official beaver reintroduction trial in Argyll was still on the Scottish Environment Minister's desk. The law – or rather the absence of law – concerning the unauthorised Tayside beavers allowed anyone at all to shoot them as long as they did not handle the carcases. That autumn, a report of autopsies on dead beavers conducted by the Royal Scottish Zoological Society showed that the shooters had been none too humane and none too selective in their targets as some had not been killed outright and others had included nursing mothers. Every additional day of the already overlong delay in making a final decision on the future – or lack of future – for Scotland's beavers was one more lump of unreasoning prejudice cemented into that centuries-old dam that holds back enlightenment and understanding and the chance of a more thoughtful and co-operative relationship with nature.

But what I did see that day was another example of nature responding to the sudden removal of beavers from the landscape. A beaver-felled ash tree had never been fully severed from the rooted stump, but rather had broken a few feet above the gnawed section and fallen into the water at an acute angle to the bank; and nor had it fully severed at the break. Instead, the area around the break was a mass of new growth and vigorous foliage, and there were clusters of new leaves all along the felled trunk. A second tree had been felled nearby and had hit the first one at right angles, and come to rest with its trunk leaning on top of the other one, and a kind of organic fusion of the two trunks had begun.

And these are tiny symptoms of the process described by David Carroll, in landscapes that have always held beavers. Here on the Earn, where the constant rise and fall of the river through spates and dry spells make life difficult enough for the beavers, they have concentrated on working behind the banks with overflows and small burns; with the occasional stretch of beaver-engineered canal and beaver realignment of the banks acting together in a grand plan that beavers can see but, mostly, people cannot. And it is here that the process of creating what David Carroll called "botanical gardens of wetland plants" will begin, any time now.

3: The Balvaig, Balquhidder Glen

The Balvaig is a short-lived river, emerging fully formed from the east end of Loch Voil, the larger of the glen's two lochs, then lazily uncoiling through a wide, flat floodplain, which the natives affectionately call Loch Occasional, given the river's occasional tendency to take leave of its senses when mountain burns and snow-melt overload it with rather more than it can reasonably be expected to transport within its banks. As Highland glens go, it is well wooded, and for much of the year it swithers between wetland and a kind of damp prairie of waist-high summer grass. I lived here for a few years and I have never really got the place out of my system. Beavers would love it as much as I do. It is one of those landscapes that really rather got under my skin. We seemed – we still seem – to have an awareness of each other.

The Balvaig veers south out of Balquhidder Glen, ducks under the old stone bridge at Strathyre then empties itself into the north end of Loch Lubnaig among alders and reed beds and nesting swans, and otters routinely grace every one of its six miles. But I think of it first and last as Balquhidder's river. Just where it nudges closest to the south edge of Loch Occasional (and where it has been known to make mischief with the single track road that creeps along the bottom of the hill there), is where the glen has acquired its most recent adornment. An old forestry plantation of spruce trees was clear-felled, then, instead of being replanted, a rare fit of environmental enlightenment kicked in and the whole hillside was left to its own devices. The wondrous – and predictable – result was a self-sown birchwood, which by late October had begun to warm to the task of drenching the hillside in colour. Flowers, songbirds, the occasional oak tree, red squirrels, pine martens and too many other natural riches to mention have adopted the place, and so have I.

Hard under the hill and right up against the roadside, and a gentle stone's throw from the river, is an old, flat-topped stone wall where I once watched a stoat in full ermine guise sprint for a hundred unbroken yards along its crest, smooth as a rolled snowball. Suddenly it leaped up, spun round in its own length, and ran back again the same distance before it jumped down onto the road and vanished among riverside trees. Now what the hell was that all about? Whenever I pass the place again I still try and puzzle it out. I'm no closer to knowing, but I'm not done yet.

Now, a rowan tree has rooted in a top-dressing of lime-green moss three inches thick. An offshoot of its root system has squeezed down through the stones until it found a gap from which it has since emerged and become an eighteen-inches-long horizontal sapling with pink leaves. I can only imagine it is some kind of kin to the

Rannoch Rowan, but this little wall has seen more than its share of miracles.

There were very fresh otter tracks in the mud by the river where I expected to find them, and a fresh spraint on a tussock at the top of the bank above the mud. What had been going on behind my back when I was examining the rowan?

The otter tracks had crossed other spoors – the prints of red deer, roe deer, heron and a small duck, probably teal. This kind of agenda-free wandering in a known landscape is how I like to engage with nature best. I stopped often to listen more intently to a sudden sound, to search the hillside in the north for deer, and there was a sea eagle around the last time I was here so I regularly scanned the middle distance and the hill skylines just in case. Occasionally I took photographs and notes. I made a pencil sketch. Most importantly, I stopped several times and sat for half an hour at a time, writing, eating lunch, or just being still, just looking, just listening.

I stopped beside a small ash tree. It was about ten feet tall, which makes it one of the smallest trees along the riverbank. There was a hole in the trunk at eye-level. It had been a place where blue tits nested, but it had been newly enlarged by a great spotted woodpecker. The tell-tale marks of its remodelling work were very visible and very fresh, so I took a photograph just for reference in case I ever wrote about it. As I focussed the camera I heard what sounded like a substantial flock of long-tailed tits. Theirs is the thinnest, highest-pitched, softest of bird calls, and mysteriously, it sounds no louder at close quarters than it does a hundred yards away. Then they were all around me, for they had swarmed into that very tree. There were thirty or forty of them and they moved through the tree like a breeze that whispered and clicked and whistled. They were so close it felt for a moment as if the sounds of their tuneless concerto were inside my head. Most of them stopped once or twice among the branches and for a second or two at a time, the nearest of them making the briefest of pauses on a flailing twig less than a yard from my face. As far as I could see, none of them fed. The whole flock's passage through the tree took less than ten seconds from beginning to end, then they flew on upstream along the bank to the next and much larger tree fifty yards away.

I was as thrilled as I was baffled. First of all, they had treated me like a piece of the landscape, which was good, and which is to say that although they had no use for me as a piece of landscape, neither did my presence cause them to change their behaviour. But then, there was this: they could have gone round the tree on either side or both sides, or (much simpler) they could just have flown over it. Instead, they chose to descend in order to fly *through* it. As they were not feeding, then perhaps it is a regularly deployed tactic to minimise sparrowhawk attack.

The incident sang in my head for the rest of the day. It sings there still whenever I pass a squad of long-tails in a wild oakwood or suburban garden or city park, wherever, and its particular significance for me is that I learned a new thing by being briefly still in their company.

There is a moral to the story too, and it is this: the way to learn about nature and to understand how it works is to spend time in its company. And it really doesn't make that much difference whether nature turns up in the guise of a flock of tits or a sea eagle or a beaver or a wildcat or a wolf pack. Both nature and we, the human tribe that likes to think it is something other than and superior to nature, prosper when something so utterly unexpected and unpredictable briefly bridges the gap between us and permits a moment of enhanced regard to cross.

⊙ ⊙ ⊙

On the way back, three drake teal leaped from the middle of the burn with that so-spectacular vertical take-off spring they have. We rather surprised each other in the same instant. I stopped to follow them in flight with the binoculars. In sunlight and at reasonably close quarters, the drake teal is a stunner: the orangey-red head is emblazoned with a metallic green leaping-dolphin-shaped eye-patch rimmed with yellow; the wings flash silver and white with a matching green flourish and the underside of the tail adds a yellow grace note. The flight is fast and erratic. As if all that was not enough, as they crossed in front of me and flew west and I panned the glasses to follow them, I became aware of the patchwork of autumn birchwood shades on the hill behind them as it moved through the background slightly out of focus, a poetic blur such as a daring film director might have deployed. Then the thing was done, and suddenly I was left with an overwhelming sense of déjà vu that caught me quite unawares.

The closest friend I ever had was a man called George Garson. He was an artist, specialising in mosaic and stained glass, and had his own department at Glasgow School of Art. He died six years ago, just short of his 80th birthday and less than two years after his wife. He taught me an immense amount about seeing with an artist's eye (although, mercifully, he never tried to make an artist out of me). A vivid memory arose of one evening when I was having dinner with him and his wife. I was trying to describe something I had seen earlier in the day on a loch in deep oak woodland. Three mallard drakes had taken off from the water, water that held all the reflected autumn shades of the surrounding oakwood. Then – as now – I had followed the ducks in the binoculars and became aware of the blurring oakwood background to the ducks' flight. When I finished the story I said to him:

"I wish to hell I could have painted it."

He slammed down his knife and fork and swore at me, neither of which he had ever done before in my company. He said:

"You stupid bastard! You just did!"

Chapter Thirteen

Sheriffmuir

ONCE UPON A TIME in a previous life forty-something years ago, I moved to Stirling and cast a speculative eye on the west end of the Ochil Hills, which rear above that ancient wee city's north-eastern corner. I was newly married and had decided that for the foreseeable future my working life would revolve around newspaper journalism in Glasgow or Edinburgh (both as it turned out) and Stirling seemed to offer a reasonable base and proximity to hills and mountains. My first exploration of these new doorstep hills was in Glen Tye, an unsung east-west glen that burrows deep into the hills from Sheriffmuir.

Sheriffmuir is best known (in as much as it is known at all) for an inconclusive battle in the 1715 Jacobite Rising in which Rob Roy MacGregor may or may not have taken part. A memorial still marks the battlefield, although any pretence at the careful dignity that still cloaks somewhere like Flodden Field, for example, has long since been obliterated by commercial forestry plantation, and more recently by the unforgiving giant strides of the Beauly-Denny pylon line, a laceration right through the heart of Scotland on a scale of intrusiveness that reaches new heights for the energy industry's capacity for bullying self-interest.

So when I creep up the steep, hair-pinned single-track road to Sheriffmuir now it requires rather more self-discipline than it did forty-something years ago. With some regret, I have abandoned Glen Tye to its 21st-century fate (which includes yet more new forestry, and it is lamentable how the planting of both forest and pylons requires miles of new bulldozed roads and concrete bridges) and found a more furtive and agreeable alternative way into the hills.

These late October late afternoon and early evening hours are apt to seduce me away from a long writing shift, and the combination of a short drive on empty roads and the spreadeagled mountain panorama from west to north puts the hills above Sheriffmuir high on my list of preferred options. A short circuit of a low hill with high expectation of meeting one of nature's most sublime haunters of the dusk is always an enticing prospect. My preferred route insists on a short, sharp descent into a small gully with a burn in the bottom and a discreet little bog to tiptoe across, like a heron on paper-thin ice, but without the option of flight if the ice cracks. I was negotiating one of its trickier steps when the underside of a whin bush exploded softly and a lumpy, shapeless cloud of tawny feathers flew out. It banked a dozen yards away to reveal itself as a woodcock flying away from me. Now that it circled low over the hillside and I could see it for what it was, I took a step back onto slightly firmer ground so that I could watch where it went, and almost stood on a second bird, which extricated itself from more or less under my boot in much the same way as the first one had escaped from beneath the whin bush. My first thought was just how close my left boot must have been to that second bird when I passed by, for I remain convinced it could not have been more than a handful of inches and certainly less than a foot.

Both birds flew no more than about fifty yards before flopping down into the long, pale hill grass higher up the burn. I considered retracing my steps to the top of the bank and edging upstream from there to try and catch up with them, but thought better of it at once, for if I disturbed them again they might well have moved on to less troublesome pastures. Besides, now that I knew that they liked the ooze and the cover of the gully, there was a chance that our paths might cross again, and I would bring a little more consideration to bear on my future crossings. It was a lovely moment, but the woodcock was not the sublime haunter of the dusk that I had in mind.

Beyond the gully the land rose and expanded into a wide, low hilltop that opened up views into the innards of the Ochils, the headwaters of Glen Tye, and the 2,000-feet bulk of Blairdenon, beyond which lay all the highest Ochils summits. There are nine over 2,000 feet and it is possible for a fit hillwalker to link them together in a single, energetic day, but mine is the persuasion that prefers them one or two at a time and at a pace that affords the opportunity of exploring some of the hills' secrets. That has been the basis of my relationship with the Ochils since the day I first blundered into Glen Tye forty-something years ago, saw a dipper on the burn there and failed over two hours to take a single convincing photograph of it. I have improved my relationship with the hills since then, and with dippers for that matter, though not my wildlife photography.

The afternoon went quiet and grey but there was a soft and pearly glow in the western sky where Ben Lomond still showed clearly. In that lucid, revealing light, and with its top 500 feet embellished by the night before's snow, it could stand in as a stunt double for Mount Fuji in a suitably low-budget film.

Near the hilltop a new movement caught my eye: a low, moor-coloured movement that crossed the hill skyline dead ahead of me and immediately soared fifty feet higher at my sudden appearance. As I don't have that trick in my repertoire I froze. It was a ringtail, the female hen harrier, the long, barred tail emblazoned with a telltale white rump patch that looked brighter than ever in the slowly gathering gloom. Having gained height she glided past at an angle to the slope and with her wings held in a very wide-angled vee, and close enough for me to see clearly the turn of her head as she took in my dark shape. I had not seen a hen harrier up here for years, although there was a time when I would expect to see one. There is no single bird in the whole of Britain that is closer to being rendered extinct by our own species in our own time than the hen harrier. It is public enemy number one in the self-interested eyes of the grouse moor mentality that stalks the high moors of the land, and seems to grow more hysterically defensive every year.

This bird that crossed my path prompted mixed feelings in me. I was very happy to see it, especially here after so many years, like an autumn-shaded emissary of the season.

I was unhappy to see it, especially here, because the reputation of heathery, grassy hillsides like these is not one that might underpin the idea of a long and prosperous life for the harrier. Maybe it was just passing through, in which case I wished it safe journey and a more welcoming destination, although it is unarguable that these are becoming very thin on the ground. But the hen harrier was not the sublime haunter of the dusk that had lured me here either.

I noticed that there was a pale, eerie brightness in the sky behind the hills to the south-east, while in the west, the pearlessence had drained from the sky and the clouds had slipped down over the mountains like nightcaps. I turned back at the hilltop and was surprised to see how little light was left in the north and the north-west.

I was almost back at the car when I finally saw nature's sublime haunter of the dusk. It was flying at zero feet, hovering at zero knots, then it lifted without any obvious gesture of its wings to around twenty feet and hovered again. It pivoted on the air and was now facing directly towards me, but its head was down; the head of a hunting short-eared owl is almost always down. It dropped in three controlled falls of five or six feet at a time, stopped again a yard above the moor, almost brushing the tips of the tallest grasses, flourishing the infinite flexibility of its wings, holding still, holding still, holding still... then nothing. It drifted away a yard, two yards back, then pitched over onto one wingtip and I could hear the soft thud of its pounce. Was that a bluff, that nonchalant sideways drift feigning indifference? The owl was up at once with nothing to show for such virtuoso stealth.

The moor had changed into its night attire in the last few minutes, the deep dark unfathomable brown of finished heather, the pale blond grasses that suddenly caught fire, a spontaneous combustion as far across the moor as I could see, but a lemon-shaded one. I turned to look behind me and a huge moon stood above the hills in the south-east. I turned back in time to see the owl hurdle the roadside fences, a fifty-yard sprint that brought it over to my side of the road with a very impressive turn of speed. Then it began to hunt again, quartering the land in the moonlight, and wearing exactly the same shades as the moor. It came closer to where I leaned against the car, perhaps twenty yards at its closest, then it thumped down again and there was a long stillness. The owl was close to the fence and I noticed a conspicuous wooden post, and thought it might appear any second with prey and take it straight to the post. I waited. Half a minute passed. Nothing doing. No owl. I looked around and found it again, a hundred yards away, and I never saw it go. I never saw that sublime haunter of the dusk rise from the moor twenty yards away. My time was done. I don't have owl eyes.

"Short-eared owl" is a name chosen by an idiot. The "short ears" are not even ears, but useless tufts of feathers. But Linnaeus knew rather more about his subject than the idiot. His Latin name for the short-eared owl is *Asio flammeus* – flaming eyes! Flame-eyed owl is what the English should have called it, because if you are ever the subject of a short-eared owl's direct stare in broad daylight at twenty paces, you will never, never forget it. The eyes really do flame. In a dusk like the one that had just drifted into first darkness, the owl eyes are smoored and there is no guessing their hidden potency.

◉ ◉ ◉

I am conscious that the image of autumn-shaded wildlife is a recurring one, but the reason for that is simply that it recurs and remarkably often. A few days after the owl encounter I had gone for a day out in these hills with my friend Garry Fraser, who also happens to be the assistant editor of the *Scots Magazine*, to which I contribute a wildlife column every month, so our friendship is professional as well as social. And, as we are both natives of Dundee, it's also tribal. Our walk began where mine had begun, high on Sheriffmuir: we negotiated the boggy gully but it proved woodcock-free that morning. And what a morning! Snow had come to the high ground of the Ochils, but the mountain arc from Ben Lomond in the west to Ben Lawers in the north was sensationally alpine, and all the land glittered with clear-skied sunlight on melting frost and iced-over pools.

We were heading up the final shoulder of Blairdenon when I heard snow buntings. There was a thin cover of snow at that height but the bleached hill grasses showed palest tawny in the strong sunlight. Now if you want to see snow buntings in such conditions what you need is one of two things. You need the birds to cluster and fly in a dense little flock for a few yards, preferably a few yards that involve flying against the sky; or you need the snow bunting flock to be so huge that it moves over the

high-plateau country like an airborne snake. Neither circumstance was in place that morning. We had stopped for
a tea break anyway, and in the absence of the sound of
our boots crunching rhythmically through the snow crust,
the thin and high-pitched voices drifted towards us from
the east. I guessed at a small flock of between a dozen
and twenty snow buntings, I imagined every one of them
clinging to the swaying tops of the hill grass, perhaps where
it grew more thickly in the lee of a peat hag, every one of
them plundering seeds, and flickering palely in short flights
from one grass stem to another, the air as vibrant with the
white flash of wings and tails as with their voices. That's
what I guessed, that's what I imagined. We saw none of it.
Not a single bird, though they were clearly within earshot
for at least ten minutes. We saw nothing because what we
were looking for were between a dozen and twenty needles in a haystack the size of the Ochils, and the needles in
question happened to be wearing exactly the same grass-
and-snow shades as the hilltop where we stood.

They were probably all males, which is the norm for
a winter mountain flock in the hills. Science thinks they
are better insulated than the females and first-year birds,
which in Scotland tend to winter around the coasts, and
it seems as likely an explanation as any. The voices of the
buntings were still there when we left. It snowed in the
night that followed, and it is quite possible that these little
mites of the Arctic tundra tholed the kind of night that
you and I might have trouble getting through.

One old autumn in the Cairngorms, with a long hill day
behind me, I wandered down the evening glen half drunk

with the sun and the snow and the unclouded skies, and I saw a large flock of snow buntings wheeling across the lower glen. I put the glasses on them and made a rough count of 200. Then, in a wide sweep of the glasses I realised that the flock was the head of a more or less unbroken mass of birds that stretched for a quarter of a mile. I took to the bed of a burn using its sound and its banks to cloak my approach, and settled against a boulder as the first of the flock passed across about fifty yards in front of me. The conversation of the flock was a roar of soprano whispers. I checked my watch. The whole flock took two and a half minutes to pass my rock. The sight and the sound of what may have been a thousand birds can still swim back into my mind whenever snow buntings chance to cross my path, and whether I actually see them or not.

Chapter Fourteen

Return to
Glen Finglas

GLEN FINGLAS RUNS THROUGH my nature-writing territory like a mountain burn of pure, clear spring water, a source of light and life and optimism. In the dozen years or so since Woodland Trust Scotland recognised the potential of the place (a potential well concealed by thoughtless commercial planting and overgrazing on the high ground), I have watched its transformation into a burgeoning Highland Edge forest of native trees with admiration and amazement. The crucial factor that persuaded the Woodland Trust of the possibilities here was that there were enough scattered remnants of native trees on the 10,000-acres estate to provide a local seedbed for new planting and natural regeneration. My admiration arises from the vision that was brought to bear, my amazement from the scale and the speed of the transformation. Whenever and wherever humankind provides opportunities for nature on this scale, nature never needs a second invitation and sets to work with a will.

It should go without saying that, all other things being equal in such a place, autumn is its finest hour, and throughout my travels in the cause of this book, Glen

Finglas was my default setting, the destination for long days in wood and on hill, for half days when whole days were not possible, and for snatched hours with a late lunch and a notebook just for the sake of being away from the writing table for a worthwhile break. It was in the latter context that I had turned off the main path to visit the waterfall after a night and a morning of heavy rain and suddenly brightening afternoon. The waterfall is tall and slender, and quite surrounded by thick foliage of mostly oak, some alder and birch and rowan and a couple of conspicuous hollies. Its voice had acquired a gravelly bass during the downpour, and scraps of rainbows jigged and reeled in the midst of the fall. Then something moved in the oak trees on the far side of the gorge that accommodates the fall. At first there was nothing more than a glimpse of dark reddish-brown and a brief flourish of black, and because the sides of the gorge are so steep and so thickly wooded it was not clear to me whether I had seen an animal climbing up between the trees, or something inside the trees, and I was just beginning to concoct a pine marten theory when a very substantial male red squirrel appeared among the outer reaches of the oak branches.

This is good red squirrel country and I see them often, but never have I seen such a stallion of a beast as that one. The traditional "red" pelage was strikingly dusted in patches of a smoky, purplish black. There was a wide band of it across his back, and another narrower band of the same shade across the top of his head that spilled down to make irregular patches on his cheeks, and there was yet more of the same on the tips of his ears. His nose was so pale it was almost white, and a matching slender ring surrounded each eye. A ruff of bright orange caught the sun on his neck, and was matched by his forelegs. His belly was bright white, and there was a curious shade of pale red behind his ears and nowhere else that I could see.

But the truly memorable feature of this squirrel that the field guides will characterise as "red", was his tail. It was full and bushy and longer than its owner's body, and it was almost jet black. When the animal perched erect to feed, it hung vertically below him like a cosh. But when he reached out with both front paws to pluck a trio of acorns on a single stem, the tail swung into the air in the shape of a tall "S", or a wonderfully rearing cobra. He was in my sight for fully five minutes before he simply disappeared into the innards of the oaks. I have been greatly entertained by red squirrels in these woods and throughout the Trossachs, but this one was so startlingly beautiful that I believe I could pick him out in an identity parade.

⊚ ⊚ ⊚

Here and there in the lower woods there are wooden benches with views, and usually they commemorate the life of someone who loved the place. One such, where I pause often, has a little plaque on it honouring the life of one William Butler, so of course I call him Yeats and recite in his memory (I have no idea who he was but I have cause to be grateful for his bench) Yeats's little masterpiece, *He Wishes for the Cloths of Heaven*, the one that begins:

Had I the heavens' embroidered cloths
Enwrought with golden and silver light,
The blue and the dim and the dark cloths
Of night and light and the half light...

The view embraces a wide, steep-side swathe of the Glen Finglas woodlands that tumbles all the way down to the shore of Loch Venachar, and to a wide, enticing wetland at the loch's western end. Every time I explore it from high above with binoculars I tell myself that in the wildly unlikely event of my being in charge of the Loch Lomond and the Trossachs National Park, I would have had beavers in there ten years ago. As it is, the park has re-introduced nothing more controversial than water voles...

Beyond the loch is another large area of wooded hillside, lower hills than Glen Finglas, with unseen Lowlands beyond them, and if you were to draw a line on a map of Scotland to delineate where Highland meets Lowland, it would cross that hilltop. All the way west from here to Loch Lomond is an area of the national park that has begun to market itself as The Great Trossachs Forest, a partnership of Forestry Commission, Woodland Trust Scotland and RSPB that has the potential to work wonders for nature, as long as the public relations effort is matched by bold conservation initiatives on the ground.

Halfway down the hill from William Butler's bench, a tall larch tree stood out from the self-sown birchwood throng, a survivor from the old spruce regime, and surviving in some style at that. Science is getting a bit picky when it classifies the European larch as "non-native" as it has been dignifying the British landscapes since 1620, although it was something of an oddity until James, the 2nd Duke of Atholl, championed its cause in the first half of the 18th century, and the apotheosis of all Scottish European larches still stands where he planted it in the grounds of Dunkeld Cathedral. But it was the 4th Duke who achieved ubiquity for the larch by planting (so it is said) seventeen million of them. I think after 400 years it has earned the right to be native. My branch of the Crumley tribe has only been in Scotland since the 1830s, having washed up in Dundee from Donegal, but it is a brave and foolish man who classifies me as non-native to Scotland. The least we can do is extend the same generosity to the European larch.

When you see them thousands of feet up and framing glaciers and 10,000-feet summits in the Alps, which is their original homeland, you understand that they are true mountaineers at heart, which may be why this solitary larch looks so at home in Glen Finglas. It is a very one-sided tree: all its branches tend southwards on its south-facing slope, a tendency that was encouraged by its youthful determination to fight for its share of sunlight in its prison of spruces. In their absence it has soared and prospered and the more considerate birches whose company it now keeps allow it the space it deserves. The trunk, which must be about seventy feet by now, accommodates a distinctive southward kink in the middle, beyond which it returns to the vertical. Its two oldest limbs established themselves at a gentle upwards angle out from the trunk, but eventually curved spectacularly into parallel vertical thrusts of their own, and their branches continue to spread the reach of the tree out into the Highland airspace.

Oak and willow gather round too, though in much smaller numbers than the birches, and all of these are brushed with the citrus shades – lime green, lemon, pale orange – to which the larch contributes sunlit gold. One of the consequences of Woodland Trust Scotland's restorative attitude towards Glen Finglas has been the return of black grouse, the one you might call the not-so-famous grouse, and sitting here in the late spring I saw a small raiding party of these handsome birds gather in that larch tree, for they are partial to the young flowers. The dashing nature of their flight ended abruptly when they landed in the tree, and folded themselves into a compact shape that resembled nothing so much as a tea cosy – a trick it shares, incidentally, with beavers.

◎ ◎ ◎

I was back in the glen on the last day of October. A weather pattern had begun to set in over the last few days – drenching nights and mornings of rain, then the sun roused itself blearily about noon and the afternoons would emerge like new butterflies. Walking up from the car park through the oakwoods, I abandoned the path to follow a burn that had grown muscular and darkened in response to the new rainfall, and where it normally bounced among rocks in tiny, pretty falls, it now slavered whitely there with all the bravado of a badger cub that has just reached that point in its first summer when it discovers that, instead of running away from every conceivable shape and shade of disturbance, it turns to hiss and face down the darkness, and discovers the strength and courage within that make its tribe the most fearless in the wildwood.

The forest here is studded with standing deadwood, a sculpture park of the fantastical. Its most impressive specimen is a broken, bare oak that dominates a small clearing: its trunk is straight and devoid of bark for about ten feet, then kinks left, then right then left again as it climbs, then tapers into a series of thin, pointed, broken-off branches, the nett effect of which is a praying mantis on stilts, or rather on stilt. I had stopped to photograph it and write it down when a patch of vivid white moved among the uphill trees. Nothing else in the oakwoods is that shape and that shade of white. It was a rear view of a roe deer, head down and feeding. But no roe deer has its head down for long, for they are the wariest of creatures, and despite my best efforts at silence and stillness, its head suddenly came up and round to look back down its spine, a long and questioning stare directly at me through a screen of saplings. Then, over ground strewn with old tree roots, sudden bogs, fallen trees and rocks, it bolted flat out and fluent and never put a foot out of place, and nor for that matter did its fawn, which I had simply not seen, but which did not need its mother's gruffly-barked instruction to follow. All of which also applied to the second fawn, also unseen by me until it broke cover, despite being twenty yards closer.

Part Three

November

Chapter Fifteen

The Ploughman's Apology

I HAVE NEVER MUCH APPROVED of Burns Suppers. In particular, they create a microclimate that insists that you read Burns in January, and only in January; a microclimate that ritualises a recitation of *Address to a Haggis* as an essential element in the annual celebration of the poet and his works, when any rationally compiled list of his best 100 would exclude it. And besides, one of the high-water-marks of his genius, and a moment of almost sacred significance to a Scottish nature writer, belongs to November. I know it belongs to November because it says so, right there in the title: *To A Mouse, On Turning Her Up In Her Nest With The Plough, November 1785.*

The verdict of posterity has judged it among his best works, and I agree with that verdict. And why should it be of sacred significance to a Scottish nature writer? Because of the second verse. Almost the entire poem is written in Scots, which by common consent – and the verdict of posterity – is his natural voice. But the second verse is in English. Burns would do that from time, and it seems to me that he deployed an occasional foray into English to indicate that he was trying to reach a wider audience as well. The second verse of *To A Mouse* is an apology, an apology to the mouse and through the mouse to all nature, an apology on behalf of all humankind for screwing up the planet. It is perhaps the very first utterance of the kind of thinking we now call conservation:

I'm truly sorry man's dominion
Has broken nature's social union,
And justifies that ill opinion
Which makes thee startle
At me, thy poor earth-born companion
And fellow-mortal!

The significance of that apology only grew on me slowly, but when I eventually tumbled to it, it began to intrigue me, and I began to read more thoughtfully his poems about nature. Somewhere in the exploration of that astounding body of work, the idea of what follows fell into place.

The Ploughman's Apology

IT WAS NOON and the high field was half done. Young man and old horse turned the plough in a sweet curve at the top of the hill where the field nuzzled into a wood of birch and pine. He called a halt. At the sound of his voice she stopped dead where she stood. He spoke compliments in her ear for the morning's labour. The newly opened earth, rich and dark red in November sunlight with the questing gulls in it like pockets of quartz, stirred in him a kind of likeable melancholy. He could smell the sea wind up here, a salt edge to the earth-sweetness. He looked down to where the furrows gathered at the foot of the hill, to where the field tilted seawards. The sea was far off and pale and flat. He did not see it well, for his long sight was not keen. He was better at short and middle distances, the ploughman's terrain. Besides, he was neutral to the sea, for it played no part in his life. He never wrote about the sea. It contributed to his life only the notion that Ailsa Craig was stone deaf, and he would write that down. Arran's mountains lay on their backs and dreamed. He had never been there. He would never go there.

But there were times when these parcels of land, the climbing acres of his father's farm, wrapped warmly round him, not like the embrace of a woman (a dark smile, Jean, the hayloft), but rather something firmer and anchoring. At such moments he felt more like a moving fragment of the landscape than a man, and he could lose and forgo himself to Nature. The land itself was his true mistress. He revered it and all the poor earth-born companions of nature with whom he shared it.

A brown hare loped easily up the unploughed stubble towards him. It stopped suddenly and sat back, staring at the horse, with ears black-tipped and tall. The horse stared back. The hare's nose told it about the horse, but not about the man who stood behind her head, watching. The hare came on again, stopped and sat again only a few feet away, ears and eyes and nose full of the horse's huge, grey presence, scrutinising her stillness. Then the horse lowered her head towards the hare and snorted, and it ran for the long grass at the field edge and its hind feet thumped the stubble as it ran.

The young man tried to remember the detail, tried to write it down in his head (he could do that, he had that gift): the dark gold eyes, round and protruding; the surprising ears; the short front legs and the small feet, but the folded power of the hind legs and the big, thumping hind feet; when the animal loped it seemed to tip forward because of the imbalance of the legs, but when it ran the hind feet reached far beyond the front feet, the ears flattened back along its spine and there was nothing faster across fifty yards of stubble field.

Man and horse ate their midday meal where they sat and stood, and the sun was briefly warm and the wind fell away. His head was half-full of poems, half full of that love of the land, ploughing the high field, with only the old grey and Nature's passing travellers for company. He loved the hares, and the moles, foxes, badgers, stoats and weasels, the lapwings and the curlews, skylarks and sparrows, blackbirds and thrushes, the crazy laughter of the green woodpeckers, the dusk anthem of the rooks, the hovering and the haste of falcon and hawk. He loved all of them without wondering why.

But he was less than tolerant of people who killed them, any of them, although he had been taught by his father not to grudge one particular poacher his bag; he thieved little enough and the poor wretch had to live. His father would shrug at his comings and goings and mutter: "A daimen icker in a thrave's a sma' request, lad." But the honourable exception of the poacher apart, he had been moved by the hare's confiding closeness to glower in his mind at those who did kill animals and birds when they had no

need, some who were less than accomplished at their killing games and simply wounded their quarry and left them
carelessly to their fate, and he cursed by name some who
were friends of his father, farmers themselves who would
greet him with a cheery wave if he met them on the road.
Few took pains to conceal their hatred of crows and foxes,
and they told stories about foxes that could make a cow's
milk turn sour, stories they had heard from their fathers
or their grandfathers about wolves that stole bairns from
their cradles, and what was a fox but a scaled-down wolf?
The wolves were gone from the Lowlands, but the sense
of them lingered on in the old folk, and some said they still
roamed the Highlands at Rannoch or Rothiemurchus or
Caithness and Sutherland, unchancy beasts that inhabited
unchancy country.

He wondered how he might feel if a wolf were to howl
now from his wood and stand there in the shadows watching him. He spun round on some mad impulse and stared,
but the only eyes watching him at the top of the field were
the hare's. He smiled at his own daft daydream and readied
the horse for the afternoon's work. He thought he might
like the wolf and keep its presence in his wood secret. He
imagined how he could conceal his knowledge from certain of his neighbours. There again, if it took to howling
in the wood at dusk, they'd know soon enough. The old
folk said the howl of a wolf could travel five miles across
open country. Mind you, they also said that the sound of
it made you pee blood, and he didn't believe that either.

For a while then, as the horse led him up and down
the new furrows, his frame of mind was not hitched up to

the work. Instead, it fumed around the names and faces of those he considered to be the enemies of Nature, the ones who treated Nature with contempt as though somehow they were above it. Then quite suddenly it occurred to him that one of the joys of working the land with the horse was that Nature relaxed in her company. A man alone was mostly Nature's enemy, but a man with a horse was just a horse in Nature's eyes, and the ancient bond between man and horse was as a bridge between the ways of men and the ways of Nature. He spoke his gratitude aloud to the horse's monumental grey rump and permitted himself a slow smile.

But his mind, in its wandering, had drifted away from his father's first commandment, the one he had first heard from his father's lips as a boy of four or five, and surely a thousand times since: "The ploughman's job is aye the next yard." That early afternoon, yards and yards passed unobserved, and while the horse was as careful and thoughtful as ever, the ploughman was distracted and less discerning. And then there was a sound that interrupted the rhythm of the toil, and a slight drag on the blade, and the man was startled back to the job in hand. He now saw that the last yard had accommodated the winter home of a harvest mouse. The plough had gone through it, and the mouse, harbouring God knows what terrors, sped away among coarse grass stalks and stubble.

He stopped the horse, which stood and looked back. She had stepped carefully over the nest. Any one of her huge feet could have stamped nest and mouse into the earth, but her eye was where it should have been, on the next unploughed yard. He spoke aloud for the benefit of the mouse, which he could no longer see:

"I'm sorry, mousie, I'm truly sorry."

He knelt beside the ruins of the nest, and surprised himself when tears edged into his eyes. He knew the ways of harvest mice well enough, how they weave a spring nest for the new family among the grasses and corn stalks, a perfect orb suspended off the ground. He had tried to write that down more than once and discarded the results, but he sensed too that there was a poem waiting to be written to a mouse. The winter nest is different, longer than it is high, and snugger with wads of moss. Now he felt the wind pick up and saw it strew the broken walls across the newly turned earth. There would be little enough left now for the mouse to build a new nest, and December was just over the hill.

The horse jerked at her harness, impatient for movement, puzzled by the unexpected pause. But the man was troubled by the moment, by his lack of vigilance, by this new trampling of Nature underfoot. His own horse had shown more respect for the mouse than he had himself. If he had shown the same respect, if he had been doing the job properly, he would have seen the nest and avoided it.

The mouse had not asked much – a few dead leaves and pieces of grass and stubble and moss, all the defence it would need to thole December winds and the cranreuch that sometimes stole in on the high field at night and whitened it before dawn. He remembered his father's tolerance of the poacher: "A daimen icker in a thrave's a sma' request."

"Not as sma's the mousie's," he muttered aloud.

He rose, sighed, spoke to the horse: "Hup, Maggie!" and he watched the stubble yield to the plough, yard after yard through the afternoon until the failing light signalled an end to the day's labours. By then, the rituals and rhythms of the work had re-established something of his character-istic good humour and as man and horse set off for home, he allowed himself to think in a more relaxed way about where he might stand in Nature's eyes. He loved that time of the day when the work was done and the homeward journey was all that stood between him and the pleasures of the evening: a meal, a drink or two, his Jean, his paper and ink. Sometimes, these days, the poems rose in him unbid-den and it was all he could do to keep pace with them. Jean liked that in him and she was not the only one.

He loved the Englishman Thomas Gray's *Elegy Written in a Country Churchyard*; he saw so much in it that was relevant to his own time and place and circumstances. It painted the land as he liked to paint it himself; he *was* the homeward-plodding ploughman. He spoke some of the verses aloud to the slow rhythm of the horse:

Now fades the glimmering landscape on the sight
And all the air a solemn stillness holds,
Save where the beetle wheels his droning flight
And drowsy tinklings lull the distant folds.

Save that from yonder ivy-mantled tower
The moping owl does to the moon complain
Of such as, wandering near her secret bower,
Molest her ancient solitary reign.

The *Elegy* was also an anthem to people like himself, who he saw as the backbone of the land, the honest men, though e'er sae poor:

> *Let not Ambition mock their useful toil,*
> *Their homely joys, and destiny obscure;*
> *Nor Grandeur hear with a disdainful smile*
> *The short and simple annals of the Poor.*

He stayed in and wrote that evening. He was quiet and self-absorbed. His father watched him for a while. His mother watched his father watch him. A tension crept into the room, a web that slowly bound the three of them together. Eventually, after several raised-eyebrow promptings from his mother, his father asked him:

"What are you writing, lad?"

"Oh, it's a mess. I think I have one verse right, but the rest is… a mess."

"Gie us the verse."

"It's not the first verse, mind, at least I don't think it is… maybe the second."

"Gie us it anyway. We'll mak allowances, won't we Mother?"

She nodded, first at her husband, then at her son.

"Go on, Rob."

"The one good verse is this:

> *I'm truly sorry man's dominion*
> *Has broken nature's social union,*
> *And justifies that ill opinion*

184

Which makes thee startle
At me, thy poor, earth-born companion
And fellow-mortal!"

His father frowned, then said:

"It's very... English."

"English?"

"Hmm, the language is very English. It's no' written by the Scots tongue in your heid, lad."

"Oh, it's a Scots poem alright. The rest of it... the mess... is a' Scots. There's twa lines here you'll like:

A daimen icker in a thrave's a sma' request;
I'll get a blessin for the lave and never miss't."

His father smiled:

"Well, I see you've been paying attention to your auld man."

His son said:

"But I want to apologise on behalf of every man and woman alive and dead, so the apology's more formal, aye – English, I suppose. Maybe I want people who know Gray's poem to read it too? If Gray were alive, I'd want him to read it."

"Ah. Well, that's a deep furrow you're trying to plough. So wha's the apology for? God? Nature? Has the mess got a title?"

The young man read from the page:

"The title is *To A Mouse, On Turning Her Up In Her Nest With The Plough, November, 1785*. Or maybe just *To A Mouse*."

"You want to apologise to a mousie?"

"Aye, and through the mousie to all Nature, and through me from all men and women."

"Hmm, what do you think, Mother?"

"Oh, I prefer *A Red, Red Rose*," said his mother.

⊙ ⊙ ⊙

Robert Burns is for all months of the year, all seasons, all years. His relevance only deepens. His humanity and his adherence to the spirit of nature co-existed within him and his poetry in a way that is very, very rare in the 21st century. His rage against the shooters who wounded a hare that limped past him on its way to find a final shelter and die from its wounds, is a symptom of the essential truth that some things have not changed very much in the Scottish countryside in the 220 years since he died. The reckless shooting of hares is a symptom of 21st-century land use too, and the impotent rage of the conservation age in the face of the worst excesses of what passes for land use policy, is mirrored in Burns. He was of his time and he was ahead of his time. He understood eternal truths and he articulated them with potency and beauty. But we, his descendants, pay him the lip service of the thing we call literature, we lend an appreciative ear to his eloquence, and we turn a blind eye to what he showed us, to his unambiguous warnings.

The poem you never hear at Burns Suppers, doubtless because it makes too uncomfortable listening at what are essentially social gatherings, is *On Scaring Some Water-Fowl in Loch Turit*. Look it up. I dare you.

Hugh MacDiarmid, at least arguably the best we've seen since Burns (although the gulf between them is so wide as to be immeasurable), put it thus in *A Drunk Man Looks at the Thistle*:

> *Rabbie, wadst thou wert here − the warld hath need,*
> *And Scotland mair sae, o' the likes o' thee!*
> *The whisky that aince moved thy lyre's become*
> *A laxative for a' loquacity.*

The land has always reached out to poets. Nature kept finding Burns. He often composed a poem in whole or in part while his hand was on the plough, when a kindlier, more compassionate agriculture held sway, and country folk leaned a little closer to nature. There were still extinctions, of course. Burns might have lived − just − to hear about the last of the wolf, and the beaver was gone long before he lived. If he had lived anything like the allotted span of three score and ten, he would have overlapped the beginnings of the Highland Clearances, and what might his muse have made of that?

I tumbled some of these things into a poem that became a kind of commission from nature for one more poor earth-born companion and fellow-mortal.

Instruction for the Bard
Take this to the Bard.
Tell him the land is empty
of Gael and wolf,
their song and howl

cut from their throats
by the nature
of their banishment.

Tell him the land is empty
of bright, wind-sighing trees
and of beavers, denying it
the slow ebb and flow
of beaver-laboured
forests and waters.

Tell him the land is full
of grey silence
and black, birdless forests;
of copses of steel trunks
branched with scythes
that slash open the air.
(These make red foliage
of mist-blinded swans
and eagles, fallen litter
of flesh and feather.)

Take this to the Bard.
Have him make a requiem
for eagle, swan, songbird,
bright tree, beaver, wolf,
Gael, song, howl, and all
the anthems of the land.

Chapter Sixteen

The Morning After
I Almost Killed a Man

NOVEMBER DAWNED CLOUDLESSLY and stayed that way all day. It was perhaps the most delectable day of the whole autumn. I was never so in need of such a day because I was carrying around in my head a black cloud the size of Ben Nevis, the aftermath of a moment the evening before when I almost killed a man.

I had been out that afternoon in the oakwoods at Kilmahog near Callander, where there was a curious atmosphere after yet another night and morning of heavy rain. By mid-afternoon it was eerily warm under a thickly padded quilt of grey cloud. Despite the temperature, I was struck by the sense that autumn had turned a corner. The woods were suffused with the constant drip and drift and sigh of falling leaves, as though the onslaught of the rain had been the final act of their tree-born lives. The canopy suddenly had the spaciousness of spring, and not for the first time I was impressed by the notion of autumn as the beginning of nature's life cycle, not an end.

Between the path where I walked and the woodland slope to the south (almost all oak, some birch and holly), the gloomy sparseness of the foliage that still clung to the trees had the feel of a pale, auburn mist, a detail of autumn I had never seen before. Perhaps it was a fluke of this tipping point day in autumn's story coinciding with so much moisture in the air, and I wrote a note to myself that said: *This intense scrutiny of the physical symptoms of autumn is revealing hitherto unseen shades and subtleties.* The observation pleased me. Was that not the whole point of writing a book about autumn this way?

Then, in birch saplings near where the Leny powers through a shallow gorge in a rock-trembling surge of a waterfall whose impact is more horizontal than vertical, and just after I had noticed a peculiar hint of pink in a patch of finished bracken, I found a very definite and deeper variation of the same shade in patches on birch bark that completely encircled the trunk. I have no explanation for the effect, but it was extraordinarily beautiful.

I paused beside a nearby oak because the base of the tree and its roots were happed in a sumptuous fleece of moss. I put my hand in to see just how deep it was and it disappeared up to my wrist. I have quite big hands. From the tip of my index finger to my wrist is nine inches. Such profusion engenders its own fertility, the products of which included two rowan saplings, four hollies, dozens of fern leaves, wood sorrel leaves and honeysuckle. It has occurred to me before that, given the great many holly saplings that spring from the shelter of oaks in this wood in particular, there are very few holly trees. Do they get eaten? (Thinks: what kind of masochistic beast eats holly leaves?) Or do they simply struggle to compete for the resources of moisture and sunlight they need to get off the ground? On my way to the Falls of Leny I must have passed a hundred inches-high saplings, and just four fully-grown trees.

The falls were in thunderous mode. The rain had swollen the river and loosened unmeasurable quantities of mountain snow. I once stood at Ardnamurchan Point watching the effects of the tail of a hurricane lash the land into submission. The falls reminded me of that sea as they crammed through the gorge and simply roared. I stood the din for five minutes, after which it began to be not magnificent but oppressive. It was as if I was being commanded to move away. I tend to listen to nature at such moments and take its advice. By the time I had rejoined the main path through the woods there was an intervening bank between me and the falls that subdued the sound to a background grumble, and I started to become aware of other sounds again – my own feet, long-tailed tits, the flutey notes of a pair of bullfinches.

Back at the car I wrote down *End of October* and underlined it twice. I was wrong.

By the time I had reached the main road along the south side of the Carse of Stirling the light was more or less gone. There had been patches of low ground mist, and although I had left these behind, there were light showers and the evening was very gloomy in the very last of the light, so I had dropped my speed to around forty miles per hour even though the road is mostly straight and the traffic was light. I noticed a car about a hundred yards ahead parked on the other side of the road with its hazard lights flashing. That's all there was. People do that for all kinds of reasons, usually because they have stopped to take a phone call.

I was much closer to the car when its headlights started flashing as well. Almost at once, my own headlights picked up something substantial lying on my side of the roadway, and I swerved across the middle of the road to avoid what proved to be a motorbike. Immediately, there was something else lying on the other side of the road, but in avoiding the bike, I was now heading straight for it. I tugged the car left again and missed – by inches – the prostrate form of the motorcyclist.

Under the circumstances, I was surprised at how well the car had handled, for small 4x4s are better known for their off-road qualities than their handling. What startled me as I brought the car to a controlled stop some way down the road was the overwhelming sense of the presence in the car throughout the incident of the best driver I ever knew – my father.

◎ ◎ ◎

The night of October 31st and the wee small hours of November 1st were haunted by what-might-have-beens punctuated by very little sleep. The beauty of the morning after was the beginning of my emergence from what had clearly been a state of delayed shock. I was eager to be out, not remotely interested in driving, so I walked from the house up to Stirling Castle, which dominates utterly the town and the countryside for miles around. The volcanic plug on which it stands has been fortified for as long as people have been interested in building settled communities in safe places with commanding views over their surroundings and a river to travel easily from the sea to the heart of the country. The Forth does that better than most. My destination was not the castle itself but Ballengeich Hill that juts out to the north from the Castle Rock. There is a mediaeval playfield there, a series of terraces cut into a curve of hillside for the performance of open-air theatre. I found a seat in the sun there and tried to think about something else.

It is only a hundred yards as the jackdaw flies to the castle esplanade and its twelve-month tourist traffic, but the sounds of it all were muted and far off. Instead, the close sounds were of jackdaws, a robin, magpies and a Jack Russell terrier that came snuffling up to my feet and put its very wet and muddy front paws on my trouser legs, demanding my attention. I like quite a few kinds of dogs but Jack Russells are not among them. This one, however, had found a human with a burden that needed lightening, and I greeted it warmly enough and scratched its head, which is what you do to dogs that greet you as a long-lost friend when you have never met before. After a few seconds, in which I imagine it had decided I was not about to magic a dog biscuit out of thin air, it sauntered off and I wiped as much of the debris from my trousers as I could without a washing machine. Its owner appeared, looking as unenthusiastic about life as Robert Bruce's statue up on the esplanade perpetually glowering across the rooftops to the river, the huge monument to William Wallace (which only the Victorians could have designed) and the steep south face of the Ochil Hills. The dog's human made no response of any kind to my greeting, but shambled on, looking at his feet while the piebald rump of his Jack Russell bobbled enthusiastically among tree roots and shrubs a hundred yards away, and I liked the dog a little more than I had done before.

I walked away in the other direction, intent on seeking out one of the hill's more engaging natives – one of its sparrowhawks. This is one of my favourite sparrowhawk theatres, with vast views out along the flatlands of the Carse of Stirling that end abruptly in that arc of mountains from west to north that so defines the beginning and the end of the Highlands. I love to watch them cruise that huge sky in climbing spirals and wait there, lingering on the thermals, high and vigilant, and thrilling while jackdaws and pigeons and the autumn clouds of Scandinavian thrushes – the fieldfares and redwings – spill out over the fields immediately to the west and never know what's hit them. I was aware as I watched that hawk-watching people and Ballengeich Hill have formed a partnership as old as Stirling Castle. For hundreds of years the inhabitants of the castle walked there with hawks and falcons on their gloved wrists. Falconry is older than most aspects of our imperfect attempts at dominating nature and trying to persuade it to do our bidding. The sparrowhawk was trickier to work with than most because it is light and therefore limited, unless the falconer was particularly accomplished.

I never much cared for falconry, although I can understand the appeal of it, not least because of its historical reach. Flying one from somewhere like Ballengeich Hill with its spoor of Stewart kings, that mountain skyline, that sheer breadth of sky, would be to strut a stage of a particularly rarefied potency. Something from a timeless twilight world, in which human and natural history intertwined, might almost be within touching distance – *almost*, because that bird that you fly is diminished by the fact that it does your bidding, that it has learned to be something other than simply 100 per cent hawk. I once thought I might take a short falconry course then try and write a story about it, and see how far I got, but then I read *H is for Hawk* and met its author, Helen Macdonald, at a book festival in the East Neuk of Fife. I liked her and was fascinated by her book, but then I reminded myself just in time that that wasn't the way I worked. The hawk that mesmerises me, the hawk that thrills, the hawk that turns my head and commands my admiration is the wild freewheeler of the thermals, tilting the castle on its rock, spinning the mountain skyline on its axis, lifting my spirits as it crampons up the thermals.

For that matter, I can also thrill to the havoc-wreaker in my garden on the far edge of the town. And if, from time to time, it causes the garden to erupt and strikes terror in the bird-brain of every house sparrow within sight and sound of its appearance, and if in the process it tumbles me from my bed before I am awake, then the sparrows and I will have to live with it, because that is just the way it is. The particular eruption that woke me up belonged to two Novembers ago. I lay still for a few moments trying to rationalise the sound through the dregs of sleep. It was familiar, yet with an unfamiliar cutting edge to it. Then I came to and recognised it. Sparrows.

It had been a vintage year for house sparrows in my neck of the woods; the shrubs, the house itself (thanks to the odd loose roof tile offering ghetto-like nesting

opportunities) and a well-stocked bird feeder had con-
spired to spectacular effect. The most I counted at any
one time was sixty-three sparrows, although mostly it was
half that number. Ornithologists in many parts of Britain
seem to think that sparrows are in drastic decline. Maybe
I had them all that year. They would line up on the fence
all facing the same way, like a newsreel of a line of dusty
refugees from a desert land. They dust-bathed in the bare-
earth patches without changing colour. They panicked
en masse at the least excuse into the honeysuckle, and
moments later they clustered as thickly as grapes on a vine
around the peanuts and the seeds, the source of the panic
forgotten, if indeed there was a source at all. And all of that
unfolded to the accompaniment of a more or less constant,
more or less day-long, companionable sparrow-chatter.

The bird feeder appeared to be the centre of their small
universe, and because the windows had been open for
much of the summer, their discordant, percussive sym-
phony had drifted indoors for months now, and become
a part of the fabric of the place. There have always been
sparrows here, but not like this. That year with its late
and sudden spring-into-protracted-summer created opti-
mum conditions for wild flowers (oceans of buttercups,
knee-high forests of orchids, flowing lava of poppies),
wild fruit (blaeberries, raspberries, rowan berries in colossal abundance), butterflies (a sudden and late burgeoning)
and, apparently, house sparrows. Of course, the down-
side to abundance is that the havoc-wreakers also prosper.
So it was that early morning when the garden erupted. I
have never heard so many sparrow voices raised to such a

cacophonous pitch. As I tried to un-fog my brain and focus on the sounds of such turmoil, I realised that something was amiss. I got up and inched open the curtains. The sound came from the depths of the honeysuckle, which rocked and throbbed with sparrows in torment. But there was only one sparrow in sight. One sparrow, and one sparrowhawk, the havoc-wreaker.

The hawk was on the grass a couple of yards from the bird feeder. The sparrow was under its right foot, and it was being methodically decapitated. Sparrowhawks like their meals headless before they start eating. (I feel much the same way about eating fish.) The honeysuckle poured out its fury, without revealing so much as a single sparrow feather. Imagine the inside of that bush at that moment, the helpless, hysterical mob, huddled in the green half-light, safe for the moment as any sparrow can ever be in a land that also allows sparrowhawks and magpies and cats and peregrines and... oh, all the other small bird tormentors that nature has invented as a means of linking its myriad chains into a coherent whole. The theory is safety in numbers, except that the numbers inevitably diminish one by one. That year of all years, the sparrows could live with that – most of the sparrows, that is. The hawk was big and brown and flecked with white, still downy around the edges, the plumage of a young female. The sparrow looked like a youngster too, although it was getting more difficult by the moment for certainties.

That spectacle on the grass is one of the most frequent prey-predator encounters in Western Europe, the house sparrow and the sparrowhawk. It is as routine as the elk and

the wolf in Yellowstone, the wildebeest and the lion in the
Serengeti, one of the fundamentals of the natural world.
Just one continental study a few years ago revealed that
sparrowhawks killed eight in every 100 house sparrows in
one breeding-season month. No other cause of sparrow
mortality could improve on two out of every hundred.
Even in November there were still a few newly fledged
sparrows on the fence, wing-quivering and shouting for
food from their parents. For a bird with the eyesight and
discrimination and flight powers of the sparrowhawk, such
an unwary sparrow is the easiest of targets. The hawk tribe
knows the garden, makes regular but infrequent appear-
ances, puts into effect a well-practised ritual, launches
from a perch into a flat-out, ground-hugging approach,
pursued by choruses of abuse from every bird it passes.
The sparrows gather in an instant cloud that beelines for
the honeysuckle, but the wing-quiverer is too preoccu-
pied with where its next mouthful of food is coming from,
and too slow to react. The hawk angles up towards the top
of the fence and the sparrow is caught and probably dead
from shock by the time the hawk hits the ground.

The young hawk on the grass took her time. She worked
with her back to the honeysuckle, a pointed indifference
towards the affronted mob. Salvoes of tiny dust-coloured
feathers scattered out from beneath one vivid yellow leg.
Every few seconds the hawk paused to look up and all
around. She stared at the window each time, the window
where I stared back through the thin gap in the curtains.
The beauty of such a bird is undeniable. I reappraised the
first impressions of her plumage. She was a deep tawny

brown in that early sunlight, splashed with creamy patches. She held her body horizontally and she stood side-on to my window, so she looked long and lean and purposefully designed, from the blunt end of her darkly barred tail to the vivid yellow cere above the dark downcurve of her bill. There was vivid yellow too in the eyes and the legs. Her neck and breast plumage flowed from vertical lines of dark markings into horizontal barring, dark brown on pale cream. She was as handsome as she was taut and tense.

The honeysuckle still protested, its rage unabated. The hawk lifted suddenly, banked in a tight circle, climbed and passed the window ten feet away, with the sparrow-brown shapelessness tucked up against her tail. The whole thing had taken less than two minutes. And two minutes after that the sparrows were out on the fence and clustered around the feeder, and if any of them noticed the scatter of small feathers on the grass beneath them, it seemed to hold no meaning at all, and I wondered if the moment had already passed beyond the reach of memory. The threat of the hawk is a constant of all of their lives. Their defence against its appearance is practised and predictable (the hawk knows this, of course), the consequence of a lethal strike is the preoccupation of less than two minutes, then the thing is done and life rather than death takes over again, until the next time. I like sparrows, I like their confidence in human company (that is also true of pigeons, which I don't like: we all have our little prejudices) and their chatty conviviality. But I also like hawks. I like their aloofness, their capacity to astonish me with spectacle, the way they explode into a landscape.

⊙ ⊙ ⊙

The explosion on Ballengeich Hill came not from that
blue yawn of sky or a missile launched from the ramparts
of the castle (something of a specialist tactic I have seen
deployed twice by the resident hawks), but from the dark
green crown of a whin bush ten yards away. The path
that human feet have threaded through the whins over
God-alone-knows how many Novembers was no wider
than my shoulders. And as my jacket was a paler shade
of whin bush green and I had been walking very slowly
and stopping often, these may have determined why a
sparrowhawk plotting a low-level attack on a quarry fifty
yards away had not immediately registered my presence
ten yards along its preferred line of attack, so that it flew
down the path *towards* me. But instantly it reassessed its
strategy and bulleted vertically up into sunlight, and in
the process presented to me its entire underside spread of
wide wings, body and tail. These displayed exquisitely tai-
lored variations on a theme of black bars on a pale grey
background, with under-chin and under-tail splashes of
white, the bars bold and solid across the tail, fragmented
and flared all across the wings and ending in dipped-in-
ink primary feathers at the outermost reach of the wide,
rounded wingspan.

But it was an eye-catchingly brandished red flag to every
potential victim all across the hilltop. These included what
I now realise must have been the hawk's intended target,
for there followed the immediate high-speed evacuation
of sparrows and finches from a nearby cluster of small

trees, and which threw itself en masse into the deepest recesses of the whins. I looked for the hawk and found it a hundred feet up and climbing, thwarted by my presence, reassessing the morning, and, if the concept ever enters the mind of a sparrowhawk, cursing its luck.

My mood that day was in a strange place, reeling uncomfortably between the insistent replays of the night before and my instinctive embrace of nature at its showiest. I had been out for a couple of hours, but had travelled very little distance and I now sat down on a seat that the council had cemented into the hilltop so that it faced the mountains. I dragged my thoughts back to the sparrowhawk, and I remembered another even closer encounter in a landscape that lay at the further end of nature's spectrum of wildness; not a low, well-trodden, edge-of-town hill in the lee of Scotland's greatest castle, but a secret woodland sanctuary in the lee of the Cairngorms' greatest mountain, Bràigh Riabhach. The Rothiemurchus pinewood, which thins out as Gleann Einich begins to impose on the spirit of a susceptible walker, is another of my favourite landscapes. I like to follow the river rather than the well-beaten Land Rover track through the forest when I walk there, a nature writer's approach to that mountain land rather than a mountaineer's, for on most days now the forest and the glen are summit enough for me.

I began to emerge from the deep cover of the riverside pines and their knee-high understorey, navigating between waist-high anthills. Where the river and the main track begin to lean closer towards each other, I could see beyond the thinning trees to the expanding openness of the glen, and there beside the track was a single birch tree. It stood out because it appeared to be growing plump little pears and every now and then one would fall off and land on the track or in the heather. The illusion was rather wrecked when some of the pears on the track jumped back up into the tree.

It had been snowing, and now there was just a thin gauze of flakes and they began to tend towards sleet, and that gauze also lent a slightly surreal aura to the activity around the tree. In the edge of the pines I found a tree to lean on so that I could examine the precise nature of this mysterious fruit in the binoculars. They were not pears at all, of course. They were pear-shaped waxwings. They had paused on the tree, a substantial flock of around fifty, and they dropped down onto the track from there to drink from a small puddle that had just begun to grow a rim of ice.

Now that the flock had stopped moving, I could hear the birds' soft conversation, a single high-pitched sound like the breath of Arctic winds...*zzeeee*...again and again, and dozens of them at a time, the minimalist contact call designed to keep the flock together at close quarters. Something about waxwings looks too cosmetic. There is a blow-dried, pinkish crest, tapering black eyeshadow, a discreet touch of blusher on the cheeks, *haute couture* of tan, grey, black, white and yellow, and those daring, scarlet sealing wax wingtips that give the bird its name. Even so, they contrived to look relaxed. Too relaxed.

The sparrowhawk came from behind me, and the first I knew of it was when it twisted in flight between my left knee and the trunk of the tree I was leaning on. I heard the soft rush of the hawk through the air. When it was halfway to the tree and still flying just above the tips of the heather, the waxwings in the tree scattered, but instead of going to ground like the streetwise sparrows and finches of Ballengeich Hill, they took to the air. That alerted the birds by the puddle, but the slowest of these was barely airborne before it seemed to burst apart. There was a brief pause, a notable silence, then the hawk rose and flew low and slow into the juniper to feed. A litter of grey and tan feathers lodged in a spray of juniper was all I could find later, a fitting and typical pinewood epitaph.

◉ ◉ ◉

Back on Ballengeich Hill, sunned and daydreaming, I was roused by the sound of jackdaws. A dozen of them were fussing around the roof-line of the Great Hall of Stirling Castle, diving down and pulling out at the last second inches above the erect perched silhouette of a solitary hawk. And how many times, I asked myself, in the 500 years since James IV built the Great Hall, has a hawk – a wild hawk or a tame – perched there and weighed up its next move?

The following day, I learned that the motorcyclist had escaped with broken ribs, and I imagine he never knew that I came within a few inches of breaking the rest of him. The encounter took more out of me than I ever thought it could, and for days afterwards – and especially at night – the moment revisited me, and so, always, did the presence of my father.

Chapter Seventeen

A Storm Called Abigail

THE AUTUMN OF 2015 proved to be a benign one until mid-November when the Met Office made the bizarre decision to start naming storms in the way that the world names hurricanes, after which all hell broke loose. The first snow of autumn almost always baptises the big mountains in September. In the six years when my writing desk sat at a window that faced west up Balquhidder Glen with the graceful profile of Stob Binnein at its far end, not once did that mountain dodge September snow, nor did its higher (but unseen from my window) Siamese twin, Ben More. Both are the better part of 4,000 feet, both are wide open to east and west and north-west winds, and both seem to catch snow earlier in the autumn and hold it longer than anywhere else south of Ben Nevis. But in the autumn of 2015, it took until the middle of November, and the arrival of a storm called Abigail.

Abigail was preceded by skirmishes between big winds and troublesome rains, the support act to the main event that more or less set the tone for most of the winter that was to follow. There were immediate implications for the trees on my reasonably regular morning walk. Take, for example, a beautiful big ash by the bridge. In the last few days it had shed perhaps a third of its leaves, leaving an airier, sunnier canopy. And the leaves had begun to change colour in a remarkable way, for they paled to a shade of bright green that embraced a hint of yellow but never became yellow. Rather, it resembled nothing so much as a tree full of sunlight. And on the grass the fallen leaves gathered in a pool of the same shade. The tree stood in its own slowly thickening and widening pool of green sunlight.

No phase of leaf-fall endures for long, and there was a sense of fluttering fragility for a few days as the pool deepened and the canopy lightened and brightened, but then there came one night of big winds and the next day the tree was utterly bare. After the two days of heavy rain that followed, the "pool" was dark brown and the few feet that use the path had reduced the leaves there to something the colour and consistency of French onion soup. And then the Met Office (whose very existence I had never given much thought too before, but which now assumed a sinister presence in my life) announced the imminence of its first-ever named storm. They christened it Abigail and suddenly the news bulletins were full of weathermen and weatherwomen beaming like proud parents and explaining the significance of the new christening policy, which I confess still eludes me. And as Abigail trundled in from the Atlantic she was depicted on our TV screens with worrying weather-map swirls straight from Van Gogh in his maddest Wheatfield-with-Crows phase, and with isobars packed tighter than beans in a bean-can, and she was accompanied by those colour-coded Met Office warnings that skipped quickly through yellow and amber to red, which indicates prepare-to-meet-thy-doom.

Well, the wind topped ninety miles per hour over the Western Isles and Shetland, Abigail dumped snow on the mountains, the windspeed on Cairn Gorm gusted to 120, which is not that unusual at 4,000 feet in autumn and winter. (The record gust of 194 miles per hour was achieved by an anonymous storm in 2009.) There were storms along both the Atlantic and the North Sea coasts, but it looked as though, in the middle of the country, the earth had failed to move. On the other hand, walking out past the big ash from where a wide view of the Ochil Hills revealed new snow down to about 1,500 feet, the thing that impressed me most was the change in the air. It was not just that it was colder, it had been supercharged by Abigail's icy breath, and she had dragged along in her wake an untidy brawl of camp-followers, wind-driven squalls of rain, sleet and snow that bashed holes in the clouds through which sudden suns scattered fast rainbows. All this seemed to have energised clouds of birds, especially freewheeling jackdaws, their voices ricocheting through the squalls like bullets. And where the path follows the edge of a wood, the sunlit edge was crammed with small birds keeping their heads down but raising their voices in unbroken, querulous chatter.

The afternoon after the morning after felt worse than the storm itself. Lured by occasional breaks in deep, dark rain, I saw an opportunity to find proper mountain snow. The small back roads of Stirlingshire were awash with prolonged deluges of water and leaves. Every small field

burn declined the culverts under the roads provided especially for them, and they burst open walls and fences and
sprawled over the tarmac, depositing bits of trees and tons
of leaves on the road, and rearranging stones by liberating
them from the insides of potholes. Abigail would prove to
be an expensive date. As I drove I wondered idly about
the Met Office's christening strategy. What if the inconve-
nienced masses of the people started to think of storms as
the Met Office's progeny, and decided to visit downpours
and gusts of spleen on it of a ferocity such as it had never
known before Abigail was conceived?

There is a forest track just off the hill road that bridges
Lowland and Highland here, and where I routinely pause
to look at a posse of the local mountains – Ben Ledi, Beinn
Each, Stuc a' Chroin and Ben Vorlich. If there was snow
to be found that day, that's where I would find it. And in
what proved to be the final respite from the rain, and the
final few moments of anything like daylight (at 3p.m.) the
lower two-thirds of the mountains emerged blearily – and
whitely! – through the murk, and I greeted them like the
father of the prodigal son. These are my snow mountains
that were lost and have been returned to me. Whatever
else might lie in store in the second half of November, my
autumn palette was finally complete.

◉ ◉ ◉

As I drove home in semi-darkness through squalls that
rocked the car and challenged the windscreen wipers to
keep up, it occurred to me that what I had seen and felt
and experienced of Abigail's wrecking spree was surely a

tiny symptom of something much, much larger, something oceanic, and beyond oceanic she was herself a small
symptom of something global. I wrote in a notebook:
Nature is restless. The next day, I drove out to the core area
of my working territory, that Highland Edge land I have
studied and written down for thirty years. I walked among
familiar woods, my favourite lochside and the lower slopes
of the mountain I know best, and the whole place seemed
to dance with wild energy. Even as I write this, I am hard-
pressed to pin down a physical idea of what I mean, and
perhaps it was more a phenomenon of the nature-writing
mind, but that's not how it felt at the time; it felt much
more like a thing of the land itself. I don't believe that the
land is neutral. I do believe that it reaches out to us, that
it is capable of a kind of language couched in terms we
might understand if only we are prepared to *listen*. It offers
guidance, a better way of coexistence between it and ourselves, because right now our relationship with it is not in
the interests of either the land or ourselves.

There is also this: the value of a core working territory for a nature writer is that over the years you acquire
a degree of intimacy, you discern recurring patterns,
you sense the rhythm to which nature moves across the
landscape, and when something new or at least unusual
appears, you are in a position to pick up on it quickly
and you can assess if its presence is permanent and how it
will fit into the landscape, or if it is transient because the
landscape will not accommodate it. The only thing I can
say with any certainty about what I picked up on that day
was that it felt like a part of something much larger than

the physical confines of what I could see and where I was walking. My response to that thought was to do the only thing that I have learned to do in such circumstances. I found a place beside a waterfall on a mountain burn with a wide view over the upper glen where young Scots pines had been hand-planted a few years ago and which now have begun to fulfil the promise of a recreated pinewood. Above it, a shattered boulderfield soars steeply to within a few hundred feet of the mountain summit. And there I sat and listened.

My ambition for that hour was to become a part of the mountain. That sense of nature in a mood of distressed restlessness was still there and, if anything, it was more marked than it had been the day before, or at least I felt it more keenly. It felt as if nature itself was approaching some kind of fundamental watershed, and again it felt that I was being confronted by a small symptom of something immense. Then, that evening, I read for the first time about Zachariae Isstrom, and I shuddered with a kind of recognition.

Scientists at the University of California (and there is a phrase I never thought I would write when I sat down to begin a book about a Scottish autumn) had just published a report about Zachariae Isstrom, a huge glacier in the north of Greenland. Remember the name, for it is surely difficult to overstate the significance of what is happening there. It is calving into the Atlantic Ocean, a force with almost limitless potential at its back to raise the world's sea levels on a scale that would make the most ostrich-headed climate-change sceptic choke on the ice cubes in his gin and tonic. It's a flawed metaphor, I know, for not even a climate-change sceptic can drink with his head in the sand, although it would account for why both his eyes would be blind to the glaringly obvious. Everything about the present and future condition of Zachariae Isstrom is going to stand climate-change thinking on its head.

The glacier is melting at the rate of five billion tons a year. The number is meaninglessly large enough to impress me. What does five billion tons of ice look like? How does science measure it? Mine must be among the least scientifically inclined of all minds. But I understand the next bit: ninety-five per cent of the sea-based part of the glacier has been "lost" (the scientists' choice of word) since 2002, and the ice is now steadily retreating inland. They then raised the possibility that the glacier will retreat twenty to thirty kilometres in the next twenty to thirty years, which means, incidentally, that it will retreat *northwards* into the *coldest* part of northernmost *Greenland*.

The scientists explained that Zachariae Isstrom is being compromised from above and below. Steadily increasing air temperature melts the top of the glacier while warming ocean currents erode the underside. "And the glacier is now breaking away and retreating into deeper ground." Nor is this an isolated incident in the north of the world, although it is possibly the largest. Besides, its near and equally huge neighbour, Nioghalvfjerdsfjorden, is suffering a similar fate, although the presence of a sheltering mountain means it is melting more slowly. But, between them, they account for twelve per cent of the Greenland ice sheet. How long before we contemplate building

artificial mountains to protect the last of the world's glaciers in order to stop our world from drowning us and all
we stand for?

Listen to what the land is telling us. Glaciers are the easiest of barometers of the world's health to read and understand. The intelligence they lay before us is simple and
unmistakeably visible. When they vanish, it is because they
melt, and when they melt, ocean levels rise and climate
change accelerates because the darker surface of the land
that replaces ice absorbs more of the sun's heat instead of
reflecting it back, the way the ice did before it vanished. I
have met glaciers in Iceland and Switzerland. I was amazed
to hear how vocal they are. We have to listen to them.

All of which made me wonder about that land-restless-
ness I detected a few hours earlier sitting by the waterfall
under the mountain in the glen of the recovering pinewood. It was as if that storm called Abigail had stirred
something slumberous, shaken up an old order into the
beginnings of something new. But it did not stop there.
Abigail was the first of a relentless series of storms that
charged through much of the winter, flaying the land
and piling floodwater on floodwater, so that when it all
finally stopped, the very land itself seemed to gasp in the
aftermath. That is what began in a quiet mountain glen
in the heart of the country and hidden among the south-
ernmost mountains of the Scottish Highlands, the same
day that a Greenland glacier made headlines all round the
world, an event that characterises the state of affairs we call
global warming, climate change, or Zachariae Isstrom or
Nioghalvfjerdsfjorden, or Abigail. And that quiet glen was

shaped by a glacier too, a glacier that melted utterly away 10,000 years ago when the last ice age's rule came to an end, when ice relented and freed up the world for new life. But what is happening now is not moving at the pace of change of the last ice age. Now we are seeing the last tracts of ice in the world diminishing *at speed*. The speed of Arctic ice-melt in the whole of the 20th century was outpaced in the first decade of the 21st. We have to listen. One way or another, I won't forget Abigail.

Chapter Eighteen

The Carse

THE CARSE OF STIRLING is the upper Forth's mile-wide, flat-bottomed valley and floodplain. But it curls up at the edges to the south, the west and the north, where hills and mountains gather round. Even the eastern end is barricaded by Stirling Castle on its rock, by the eastern "gable end" of the Ochil Hills and by the Abbey Craig with its preposterous but somehow agreeable Wallace Monument. The Forth only escapes such a noose by writhing through a berserk course of loops – "the Windings", a dozen of the most eccentric river miles in the country either side of Stirling itself. I was intrigued to observe the parallel fates of Forth and Tay as Abigail and her retinue of named storms smothered the country in floods.

The upper reaches of the Tay, with its vast river basin, gather ferocious power from overgrazed deer forest and grouse moor hillsides, and exacerbated by wind farms and commercial plantation forest, both of which wreck natural drainage and hurl water down onto the low ground through industrial scale drainage channels. Downstream, the river's course and that of many of its tributary rivers have been straightened or otherwise tampered with over the years. The Forth's upper reaches are well wooded, notably in the Trossachs, and its course has largely been left to its own devices through the Carse, where miles of loops slow the flow and mitigate against flooding. From time to time it sprawls far and wide across the grassland fields of autumn and winter, but never for long. Add beavers into the mix, with their capacity to slow watercourses and their common-sense wisdom in the matter of manipulating river systems (and they have just begun to find their way over the vital watershed between Forth and Tay just south or west of Loch Earn), and you have a useful tool at your disposal to counter some of the worst excesses of global warming with its increasing tendency towards Abigail Syndrome. It is worth pondering that every decision we have made about watercourses in this country over the last 400 years was based on rivers without beavers. We have some serious homework to do in the matter of rectifying that omission.

The Carse puts its own individualistic imprint on the landscape, a legacy of the geological and human histories that have sculpted and sandpapered the land and which lie just below its well-tilled surface. It is the corpse of a glacier, a dried out sea loch and a drained bog. Flanders Moss towards its north-western corner is a souvenir of the landscape that was, a raised bog, a National Nature Reserve that somehow escaped arguably over-zealous agricultural reforms. Nature loves it. Every time I go there, I think of the Carse as the mile-wide, miles-long wilderness of bog and wetland and woodland that must have evolved out of the ice, home to wolf and beaver and eagle, seafarers gingerly threading a course through the loops of the river, pausing under the black shadow of the volcanic plug that sat in the throat of the valley – where one day a thousand years of castle-building would begin – then easing westwards into a majestic land. Oh, to have seen that Carse then in any guise other than my own imagination.

As it is, I must have logged thousands of driving and cycling and walking miles across and along the Carse in the many years I have been its near-neighbour, and when I got round to the idea of establishing a writer's territory (an idea I borrowed from watching golden eagles a couple of watersheds to the north), the Carse was an essential component, for that meant that I would travel constantly back and forward across the Highland Edge, Lowlands into Highlands and back, and there is no richer terrain for nature in my own country than that overlapping of mainland Scotland's defining realms.

The autumn speech of wild geese on a certain watersheet under a mountain skyline and layered with the deeper grace notes of whooper swans is a cacophony of peace, especially if, like me, you incline towards the dusk rather than the dawn. Dawn dispatches the geese in a single tumultuous salvo, followed by a more or less day-long silence. But the dusk weeds them out of the farthest reaches of their feeding forays, lures them home in ones and two, in tens and hundreds, and occasionally in thousands at a time. They come in over the mountains, the trees, out of the shrouded east at your back or out of the ashes of the sunset west, and they settle in a thick, dark band of water half a mile long and gossip all night about the day's doings, about the night's dangers. And just as you think the day is done, the wind throws you a snatch of a single whooper swan, bugling home alone. There is no end to the spell of autumn nightfalls on such a loch, and your presence is limited only by the deepening cold, and by how long you can stave off the pangs of hunger and thirst. But perhaps the last thought that occurs to you as you pull out for the night is of the golden eagles you left behind you, hours ago now, in that glen beyond the first of the mountains, the adult female and her newly fledged chick on a ledge near the eyrie buttress, her mate a hundred yards away and a hundred feet higher, perched on a rock with the longest, widest view across land and sky of any rock in their home glen; that glen where the eagles taught you the wisdom of a nature-writing territory and how to unearth its secrets, its intimacies, and you saw eventually why it must embrace Highland and Lowland so that you might better understand your own place on the map.

◎ ◎ ◎

Mist flattens the land. The mountains and the foothills vanish and the Carse is defined not by their bold upthrusts but by a grey blur under a clamped-down grey hemisphere. These are the close-quartered days, the inward-facing days, and November is something of a specialist in sprawling handfuls of them across your path in slow, quiet succession. You rein in your vision, you slow your step. Or you inch the car along the empty, narrow roads among farms with window down and the heater up a notch. Sometimes, on such a day, the car is your best friend.

A big old roadside birch was already midwinter-bare in early November. A small burn beneath it defined the edge of the field. I saw bird movement right up at the crown of the tree and pulled onto the verge a hundred yards away for a better look. For a few moments after I switched off the engine I heard the murmur of the burn as it dipped in under the road, but at once it was lost under the muffled roar of several hundred wings. The tree emptied, discarded its dense foliage of fieldfares and redwings. Over the years I have developed a technique for such a situation, which is to slip out of the car while the birds are gone and open the back door (the car is a small 4x4 with a spare-wheel-bearing door that opens to the right and so helps to screen me if I watch from there). And then I can see what's going on behind, which I can't if I stay in the car.

The birds had not gone far. After about a quarter of an hour they began to drift back up into the birch. Any flock of migratory birds is restless, more often than not. Travel is their natural habitat, and restlessness is their natural state whenever they gather and perch. Three vehicles passed in the next half hour and they filled the air each time. I watched their flights. The limits seemed to be a hawthorn thicket to the north and a rowan tree halfway to the thicket, and on the other side of the road they flew to a single hawthorn tree and a telephone wire. At the centre of this whole area stood the birch and, directly across the road from it, a dog-eared old beech. After about an hour, in which small groups of birds came and went from the birch and the beech, it became clear that the day's main purpose for these birds was to pillage spilled grain from a stubble field a hundred yards to the south. Then, once I had got my eye in and begun a painstaking scrutiny of the field, I saw that they were not alone: a much larger flock was working the field from the edge of a wood to the south.

The Carse is a four-season thoroughfare for birds on the move, thanks to its clearly defined east-west course and its feeding opportunities. In a lull out on the stubble field I turned my binoculars on the hawthorn thicket, where I found these: redwing, fieldfare, mistle thrush, starling, chaffinch, linnet, bullfinch, yellowhammer, tree sparrows and house sparrows. The thrushes apart, these are the small bird natives of such a place. And on such a day, the male yellowhammers and the male bullfinches glowed in the dull light like fairy lights. In that hundred square yards where most of the bird activity unfolded, a throng of essentially grey-brown birds might not attract too much attention, but anything brightly coloured or white can expect to lodge in the eye of a speculative sparrowhawk or peregrine falcon at a considerable distance. I know the sparrowhawk is in the edge of the wood to the south, and I know the peregrine's base is a crag just up there in the mist, rather less than a minute's flying time away if he put his mind to it. And be sure that if I know it, every bird in sight knows it too. There are buzzards and kestrels to worry about too, and while these are happier hunting small mammals, they are not likely to pass up a birding opportunity if one crosses their path.

All over the Carse and on every day of the year, its vigorous and diverse birdlife is at risk from the very nature of the landscape itself – its wide-openness. The trees and the hawthorn thickets and the occasional small woods are sanctuaries, but mostly the food sources are out in the wide-open flat fields, and a predator with eyesight like a sparrowhawk or a peregrine can choose a target from a long way off and pick the best, the stealthiest line of attack. The predators' other commonly deployed strategy is to make themselves blatantly visible, to cruise the airspace and cause mayhem, and see what opportunities arise. A sparrowhawk appeared, fifty feet up, drifting with menace above the stubble field. It was still a hundred yards from the big birch when the fieldfares and redwings reacted, fled en masse for the hawthorn thicket. So far, so good.

At that point, I had been more or less still for two hours, more or less screened by the open rear door of my car, and right in the middle of the open-air theatre the birds had designated for themselves that afternoon. And then one of nature's unlikelier little dramas took the stage. Just as the sparrowhawk reached the solitary hawthorn tree in an eerily slow glide that even I found ominous (so I'm guessing it was designed to terrify the birds), there was a burst of high-octane activity at the edge of the small burn that headed towards the stubble field before taking a right-angle bend towards the hawthorn tree, which now hosted the perched hawk. Two birds were locked in tumbling, squabbling, cartwheeling combat, in which blows were struck with claws and beaks, until one of them broke free and sprinted away down the line of the burn. Immediately the second bird followed in furious pursuit. They were the unlikeliest of foes – a redwing and a yellowhammer.

I was so enthralled, not to say bewildered, by this turn of events, so absorbed in trying to keep the combatants in focus in the binoculars that I made the same mistake as they did – we all forgot momentarily about the sparrow-hawk. Just as the redwing reached the right-angle bend, with the yellowhammer a yard behind, the hawk appeared from below them, coming in the other direction, for it had used the banks of the burn for cover and flown just above water level. The redwing twisted sideways and dived for cover in the longer grass of the banks, but nothing twists sideways faster than a hunting sparrowhawk, and when the redwing hit the ground it was already in the hawk's talons. The yellowhammer flashed above them, hurtled round the bend, and inexplicably perched in the hawthorn, where it was as conspicuous as a flag on a flagpole. I switched my attention back to the hawk just as it eased into the air with the now headless redwing tucked neatly beneath it, and turned away south, low across the fields until I lost it against the background of distant woodland. It has occurred to me from time to time when I have been watching redwings that that diagnostic underwing patch of dark red looks like a bloodstain. I now know, having seen my first headless redwing very clearly in good binoculars, that redwing red is much darker than redwing blood. I turned back to the hawthorn but the yellowhammer had gone.

I turned again to look at the hawthorn thicket in the north and counted over a hundred fieldfares and redwings there. A few minutes later, they flew back to the birch tree and there were at least twice that number. There was also a pair of mistle thrushes right in the topmost branches.

Throughout the two hours, with all the alarms and excursions of the flock, these two birds had not moved. They were, I guessed, seen-it-all-before natives, and therefore immune to that restlessness that so characterises the autumn and winter lives of nomadic migrants.

◎ ◎ ◎

The interaction between predator and prey is a recurring theme of the Carse. The place is a favourite haunt of waders whenever floodwater patterns the fields with pools. Driving across the Carse on the way home from somewhere further north, and pausing often to scan floodwater pools, I saw a dark stain a long way out in the fields. It could have been anything or nothing, but the years have taught me that when something catches my eye in an unfamiliar way in a familiar landscape, it is always worth stopping for a look. If it's nothing, all that's happened is that I spent half a minute finding somewhere to stop and focussing binoculars, which is not a great price to pay. So I stopped, and the "dark stain" turned out to be more than a hundred golden plovers. I have a soft spot for golden plovers because, among other things, they embrace the lowest ground of my writing territory – like that flock in a wet field – and the highest ground, where they keep the company of golden eagles (and sometimes pay for the privilege with their lives).

There was a track nearby that headed out across the fields, and a hundred yards away there were two dead trees. I judged I might be able to reach one of these without alarming the birds, and I would have a much better view from there and I could pretend to be a piece of tree trunk for a while.

The plan went well. I made the nearer of the two trees, then chose a line that put the second tree between me and the flock that would help to break up my shape as I closed in. It took me ten minutes to cover fifty yards but eventually I was where I wanted to be and the flock was intact and feeding busily in the edges of the floodwater. Waders and wildfowl – and swans, in particular – are drawn to that combination more than any other inland situation. They appear to feel much more secure when they can feed through shallow water. Lapwings, curlews and oystercatchers all do it.

Sometimes the aesthetics of watching wildlife are simply an end in themselves. A dense flock of golden plovers in low afternoon sunlight appears to ripple as it moves, the way a high tide moves at slack water, an undulation of the surface rather than a wave, then the first hint of an inches-high surge running up the beach as the tide turns. And they are surely the most beautiful of our wader tribes. Over half an hour they edged closer to my tree until the nearest birds were only fifty yards away, and as I relished this moment of supreme birdwatching elegance, I reminded myself that this had been my "dark stain", and I reinforced my own belief in the essential ritual of taking the trouble to stop and look *every* time. Sometimes the dark stain will be a new scattering of manure on the field, but sometimes it will be a pot of gold.

Fifty jackdaws appeared from over my shoulder in a hurry, and announced their arrival in raucous chorus, and as they passed me I saw the peregrine at the top of the flock and the plovers took to the air in a single convulsion. They wheeled across the sun in a flock as tight and silent as the jackdaws were loose and chaotic. The jackdaws dragged the peregrine away with them, bullying it far out across the fields, and in their wake the plovers drifted back down within a few yards of where they had been, and every bird lifted its wings as it landed and pointed them at the sky before folding them away. But no sooner had calm resumed than the second peregrine struck a single bird on the far edge of the flock. It lifted off at once with the plover's wings thrashing the air beneath it, and landed again twenty yards away, where it pinned the plover to the earth until its convulsions stopped.

It's the oldest trick in nature's book, or at least it's one of them. The decoy flies over and allows itself to be driven off and the instant that calm resumes and the prey species is at its least wary, believing the danger is past, the second falcon strikes with exquisite timing. I shake my head in wonder at the beauty of the rippling plover flock. I shake my head in admiration of the tactical precision of the falcons. That's the way it is. Out on the Carse of Stirling, you get a better view than most places, but only if you have taken the trouble to stop.

◎ ◎ ◎

The peregrines and the plovers are but two players in an eternal pageant, their roles unchanging over millennia, the plot lines and their denouements more or less predictable. The relationship between predator and prey species is set in stone. Unless… the predator happens to be your species and mine, for we are forever thinking up new ways to torment the creatures with which we share the planet. And sometimes our own imprint on a landscape like the Carse is as unpredictable as it is unwitting.

Whooper swans like the Carse. Sometimes they settle in the same field for days, weeks if the feeding is good enough and if the field sustains half an acre of floodwater. For several days I had marked the gradual build-up of swans in just such a field until they had mustered thirty birds, and these were joined by fluctuating hundreds of pink-footed geese and a handful of Canada geese, which are part of a small but growing native population. The field was in stubble. On a day of brightening weather I found all the swans and two or three hundred geese clustered quietly around a patch of floodwater around noon. Slowly, as the sun began to warm the early afternoon, the swans stirred. A group of six appeared to reach a consensus, got to their feet in unison, and walked in well-spaced single-file towards the north end of the field, where they began to feed on spilled grain. At first the other swans either watched or dozed on, but over the next half hour they followed, a few at a time, until every swan was head-down in the stubble.

The geese were unmoved. A few bathed, most dozed. The afternoon flowed then ebbed at the same serene pace. A mist drifted in and lay above the hidden river, the tranquil, looping meanders of the upper Forth. A sparrowhawk wheeled across the field. A distant tree fired off a fusillade of rooks. The hawk ducked down and vanished at speed, watched by thirty swans. The rooks dematerialised as if they had never been.

Then a mechanical drone sounded away in the west – a helicopter engine with a deep-throated throb. It grew louder over several minutes and as it did so, the swans stood tall and listened, staring westwards. Then the geese went slowly berserk. First they all stood, not just the crowd round the floodwater but also two more large groups in the adjacent fields. Then they began to give voice, an anxious mutter that swelled to cacophony then to bedlam as the helicopter appeared low over the farm buildings. The geese rose in clouds and headed straight in the direction of my car. The nearest birds passed a dozen feet above me, the air rocked with the rasp of wings. The flock climbed and circled and called out in hundreds of voices. It was five minutes before the first of them landed again, five more before the last of them settled among the crowd at the floodwater. By then, the helicopter was lost to sight and sound, having passed well to the north. In all that time, not one swan had moved, but they added their own brassy chorus of single notes to the goose chorale, each *woop?* apparently embellished with that rising, interrogatory edge.

The sun grew almost warm. The swans resumed their feeding, the geese their loafing. There was another gentle half hour of such tranquillity before the decisive moment of the day erupted. The catalyst was another engine, higher pitched, more strident, and far more alarming for the birds – a microlight. I can only assume that it was the appearance of such a huge wingspan relative to their own and so low over the field that so terrified geese and swans alike, but I was intrigued by the very different nature of their responses. The geese flew as before, criss-crossing hordes of them, for they joined forces as soon as they were airborne with their kin from the next field. But the swans did not fly. They ran.

They ran as I have never seen swans run before. Running whooper swans is invariably a prelude to take-off, body and neck stretched horizontally, wings beating vertically. Not this time. After the first few strides the swans brought their wings to bear much as an athlete pumps his arms. Their bodies and necks remained vertical and the wings beat horizontally, not to generate lift but running speed. Thirty swans made a flat-out beeline for the floodwater, where they gathered, wading or swimming, but with their heads still high and voices raised.

Questions for the bemused swan-watcher in his car at the field-edge:

1 – The microlight engine was quieter than the helicopter, albeit with that strident dimension, and it may have been that the tone rather than the volume unnerved the birds, but did the swans misunderstand that huge fixed wing as some kind of imponderable predator, an eagle from a nightmare?

2 – I have watched whooper swans for more than thirty years, and not only have I never seen such behaviour before, I have never even heard of it. But every swan reacted to the situation in exactly the same way at the same

moment. Was there a signal? Did it specify "run – don't fly" because in that particular circumstance they considered their best option was to stay on the ground?

3 – And if so, what is the significance of a half-acre patch of inches-deep floodwater? What reassurances did that offer in the face of an attack by an eagle from a nightmare?

Answers were not immediately obvious. But sometimes, with a species you have watched so eagerly for so many years, it is good to be flummoxed. You reappraise what you think you knew, you scan the written records of others in your bookshelves to see if they have solved a puzzle that you have not, and when you draw blanks there you resolve to go out again to the field, to go back, to sit and watch again. And meanwhile, the landscape of the Carse endears itself to you a little more, and you think again how much the sum of the parts of your chosen writer's territory is exceeded by the whole thing.

Chapter Nineteen

Autumn into Winter

TREES HAVE COLOURED every shape and shade of this pilgrimage through autumn. And if your mindset is generous enough to indulge the idea of an apotheosis among Scotland's trees, it is surely to be found in the Fortingall yew, deep in Highland Perthshire. You could be forgiven for thinking that there is very little new to say about the Fortingall yew and nothing at all of any certainty. Pontius Pilate may, or may not, have played in its shade before he mysteriously turned up in the Bible to determine the fate of Christ and the course of Christianity. It may or may not be the oldest living thing in the world. It is reasonably safe to say it is 2,000 years old. But it may be 5,000 years old. Or it may be much, much older. The new broom that was the last ice age still permits the possibility that it is 9,000 years old. Nobody knows. Nobody knows because, unlike the Californian redwoods, which we know can live to 3,000 years old, yew trees die back from the inside of the trunk. Their annular rings, by which most trees can be dated, have no protective rind, so they disappear as the trunk disintegrates. As Hugh Johnson wrote in his book *Trees*, "The Fortingall tree has no centre left at all: it is a palisade of living fragments."

So, just when we thought it had nothing new up its sleeve with which to scratch our heads and furrow our brows, in the autumn of 2015 it stunned silviculture's inner sanctum by producing three berries. Actually they're not berries, they're fleshy red cones that protect a single seed, but because they are red and roughly berry-shaped, that's good enough for most of us. The thing is that silviculturists had always presumed that the Fortingall yew is male, but now it has produced three berries, and only female yews produce berries. So it would seem that one of the younger fragments of the palisade is female, "younger" being a relative term.

The phenomenon of yew trees apparently changing sex is not unknown, although it is not common either, and when it does occur, usually only part of the tree changes. But the fact that this one has done it after somewhere between 2,000 and 9,000 years of being the alpha male of all yew trees – all trees for that matter – has rather caught the fancy of the silvicultural world, not to mention people like me who just like trees a lot.

I confess I smirked an inward little smirk to myself when I heard the news. I find it so reassuring when nature catches us out and slaps us across our superior faces, so that we are compelled to revise our thinking, and sometimes when we do that, we have to hold up our hands and admit we don't know as much as we like to think we know. My own first response was to wonder if this has happened before, to this tree. It has, after all, been around for a while, and we have no idea whether it began life as a female and changed to male after, say, a thousand years.

We have no idea whether it has produced berries sporadically throughout its life. All we know is that, suddenly, within the very limited context of its recent history, this apparently male tree has grown a berry-producing branch.

I have never liked the Fortingall yew's imprisonment behind a stone wall and a locked metal gate just outside Fortingall's wee churchyard. I think it should be allowed to take its chances with all the other yew trees of the world, as it did for thousands of years before the prison builders came along. Tampering with nature, succumbing to our age-old instinct to control it, is one of the less endearing character traits of our species. In my beaver book, *Nature's Architect*, I quoted my American friend David Carroll's book, *Swampwalker's Journal*:

> *The term "wildlife management", often used in the environmental polemics of the day in reference to human manipulation, is an oxymoron. We should have learned long ago to simply leave the proper natural space, to respectfully withdraw and let wildlife manage wildlife.*

Yes we should, but the idea terrifies us. Besides, wildlife management is an addiction for which our species has yet to find a cure. Indeed, we have shown no desire to find a cure. The Fortingall yew's berries have just provided one more manifestation of the addiction, for science has elected to cut the berry branch off the tree, and to plant the berries in pots under controlled conditions. If you have not visited the Fortingall yew, you may not know that inside its prison is a little green plaque planted to commemorate the Queen's Jubilee in 2002, so that it might proclaim the yew as one of Fifty Great British Trees, and adding that it is sponsored by the National Grid. By what preposterous arrogance does anyone get to sponsor a plaque to tell the world that such a tree is "great"? And what on earth has it got to do with the Queen? And now this. One more variation on the theme of managing nature has judged that the tree is not really fit to dispose of its own berries. No storm must be permitted to prise them free and scatter them where it will. No bird may be permitted to pluck the berries one by one and deposit the seed somewhere else nearby in the time-honoured fashion. And should it still be really necessary to point out the bleeding obvious, which is that however many thousands of years have passed since the Fortingall yew sprouted from a seed, there are only two ways that seed could have arrived at Fortingall and one of them is on the wind and the other is having passed through the innards of a berry-eating bird or beast? We used to be nature ourselves once. Now, every day, we find new ways to travel further away from it than ever.

Old trees dignify old built stone in a way that is rarely reciprocated. The prison-like incarceration of the Fortingall yew (the illusion compounded by iron bars set into the high wall and a fat padlock on a robust, iron-barred gate) is as unsympathetic an interpretation of that truism as you will find. But where nature has moved in on long-abandoned human architecture and is left to its own devices, the effect is more of a benevolent regime of enhancement than the rigid incarceration of the Fortingall tendency, which denies the tree dignity.

The news from Fortingall urged me out on a mission to restore my faith in the dignifying place of trees in our midst, and in the company of the phenomenon that is Scotland's lost broch. Bit by bit and with almost divine artistry, nature overwhelms it a little more each year, and renders it a little more verdant. Strictly speaking, it is not lost at all. It has not gone anywhere in the 2,000 or so years since it was built, and it is clear from the official register of such things that the archivists of our built heritage know where it is, how high its ruinous walls are (seven feet, ten inches), its internal diameter (about thirty feet), and what details are still in evidence (three cells and a staircase, and they might have mentioned the doorway and entrance passage too, but didn't).

It stands then, where it has always stood, on a low ridge among the rippling fields of rural Stirling and just above the level ground of the Carse, which is not quite what you might expect with brochs. Their stronghold, after all, is in the Northern Isles, the Hebrides and the Northern Highlands. There are a few in Argyll, two southern outposts in Galloway and the Borders (one near Duns is a monster by the standards of anything else in the land), and there are known fragments in Angus and Fife. And then there is this extraordinary Middle Earth survivor in Stirlingshire.

I think I must be its best customer. I have never once seen another soul there, although there is some evidence that badgers go in about the place. I go several times in each season of the year, partly because seasonal transformations make it feels like four different places, four different evolutions of a kind of natural seductive magic.

And now that I think about it, the broch no longer "stands" on its ridge at all (although it did once), but rather hunkers down into its ridge. It is so smothered in vegetation, so embedded in a spacious ring of big trees, that the sparse traffic on a minor road a hundred yards away would see only a dark field edge and a woodland edge beyond. Furthermore, there is no sign, no car park, and (mercifully) no neatly clipped Historic Scotland lawns. What there is, is a farm track that crosses the ridge then dives down to the flat fields of the Carse, and as you pass the edge of the ridge's woodland there is a discreet little gate in a discreet little fence, which is why, out of respect and gratitude for whoever owns the ridge and its half-buried treasure, I have declined to say exactly where it is or what it is called.

Some places are layered with what I think of as natural sanctity, places that seem to demand respect. Every time I push open the gate and take pains to close it soundlessly behind me and step into the trees that cover the ridge, I feel the weight of an unspoken commandment: walk softly. At the very least, the footsteps you tread in are 2,000 years old, and who knows what and who preceded the broch, and for how long?

Whether by accident or design (by design in the first place is my guess, but whose, and how long ago?), the narrow, half-hearted path along the crown of the ridge and the setting and the very walls of the broch are ablaze in their seasons with thousands of snowdrops, then daffodils then the deep smouldery blues of wild hyacinths. And when all these are done and summer has thickened the walls with more moss, more ferns, more wildflowers of myriad varieties, and filled the inner space with nettles (all of this much to the delights of butterflies and bees and the sporadic raids of spotted flycatchers), then the big beeches and the sycamores and the ashes smother the place with all the fallen shades of autumn, and the two majestic Scots pines that rise just beyond the broch's northern edge promise shelter from winter's north winds. It is as if nature has decided to dress the wounds of the crippled building, and to pay its architect the supreme compliment of treating his work as an organic fragment of the very landscape where it is rooted.

When that architect set the very last stone into the top course of the broch's tapering tower, it would have stood at least fifty feet in the air above what was surely a tree-less ridge. Otherwise why build a broch on it at all? Why such a defensive structure and lookout tower of such massive proportions and so many hundreds of miles from the stronghold of the broch builders, unless it commanded a stupendous view in every direction, and (for it is widely assumed among historians that brochs were a status symbol of important people) unless it could be seen from a great distance? That great spotted woodpecker pounding its paradiddle into the topmost branches of the broch's oak tree neighbour... his is the view that the broch builders had in mind. In fact, the oak tree is a reasonable approximation of the building's height and massiveness. The most intact of all brochs, at Mousa in Shetland, survives to a height of forty-three feet, six inches, but its internal diameter is only a little more than half that of the Stirlingshire broch, so perhaps my lost broch stood over sixty feet high, in which case the oak tree is just about right.

The brochs continue to exercise historians' imagination and the best guesses of our intellect, but mostly they simply baffle us. They are routinely referred to as "Pictish brochs", for which misinformation we have Walter Scott to thank. We don't know who built them, but we know the Picts didn't. We do know that there is nothing else remotely like them anywhere outside Scotland; that they did not evolve from a humbler dwelling, but rather they were the fruits of an inventive mind, which came up with a design and then built it. It is also fair to say that that same design with its thick double walls that accommodated stairways and galleries, and the single, small and heavily defended doorway, informed much of Scottish traditional architecture right up to the tower houses of the mediaeval era. The design was a work of far-sighted genius. We just don't know whose.

So on a quiet November day, a lull between storms lit by an almost grey sun, I eased open the small iron gate, closed it (soundlessly) and stepped at once from sunlight into shadow as the trees clustered round. The ridge loses almost no height at all to the north, where small, neatly hedged fields edge away towards the distant mountains of the Southern Highlands. But to the south a steep and well-wooded bank plunges towards the flat fields of the Carse. I had walked less than fifty yards from the gate when a stoat appeared from behind a tree trunk and skipped down the skinny path towards me, the first stoat I had ever seen here. It stopped dead, stood on two legs, and tried to stare me out, as if I was an over-developed rabbit he might delude with his devilment and fell with a swift bite to the throat. I made the approved clicking and kissing noises that usually lures stoats and weasels closer, but this one was smarter than the average stoat, bounded left and vanished among the trees, and quite possibly among the old, over-grown badger holes of a cold sett, for although I lingered for a few minutes, it did not reappear. But it left a good set of footprints in a patch of wet mud.

The broch is surprisingly well hidden, and I was only a few yards away before it reared its grass-encrusted walls like a low and mysteriously curved cliff, except that here and there patches of old stone push through the vegeta-tion, and you realise that the cliff is carefully constructed in wonderfully worked stone. Patches of that eerie sunlight knifed down through the trees and lit the stone with a dull gleam. In spring, there are daffodils everywhere here. They line the terrace that runs round the broch to the south, a narrow stone ledge that peters out towards the entrance on the east side. The walls at this point are head high, and so are the daffodils – head high, shoulder high, waist high, and knee high. If you step in through the short entrance passage (as short as the combined thickness of the double wall – about nine or ten feet) into the circular courtyard, where here and there the walls reach almost eight feet high, you find daffodils dancing there too. In November it was as if they had never been, and all was submerged under a smouldering, darkening pelt of fallen leaves.

The unmistakeable cacophony of jays cut into the late afternoon quiet high up in the oak behind my back. I turned slowly in the centre of the broch's circle to look at them, and was greeted by a sight I had never seen before.

One of the jays was in mid-air, had just hurdled the wall of the broch and was approaching me at pretty well eye-level. It flashed left and passed my right shoulder so close that it left the sound of its wings in my ear, as indelible as a stoat's footprints in a patch of mud. By the time I had turned back to follow its flight, it had crossed the further wall with inches to spare and swerved away in a fast climbing diagonal between the two great pines, and there I lost it.

"And what the hell was that all about?" I asked the trees and the grown-over walls and the litter of leaves and acorns and beech nuts and pine cones. I will never know.

I am a fan of brochs. I have visited them from Shetland to Lewis to Skye and Glenelg, to Lismore, to Sutherland and Caithness and that vast Edenshall broch near Duns. I have never encountered one with an atmosphere like this. Somehow the sense of great age is more palpable because it offers itself only in fragments. The shape and stature of a broch is unmistakeable, but this one is cloaked and fattened and softened and somehow soothed by its greenery and the four-season colours of a kind of wild garden; and in the process of all that, its essential old stone skeleton is elusive. The occasional patches of bare stone are dropped hints of the structure beneath; its great age is safeguarded even as nature reclaims it. This is no longer a man-made artefact, no longer the fruits of the genius we call architecture, no longer the raw material of the science we call archaeology, but rather it has become the raw material of the science we call nature. The lost broch of Scotland may not be physically lost in the sense that it still roots where it always did, but it is in the grip of an inexorable process of reclamation by nature, it is slowly slipping out of the unnatural world of man and his built works, and back into the natural world which is, after all, the source of everything.

⊙ ⊙ ⊙

Most mornings of the working week when I am at home, the walk between my house, the shop where I buy newspapers and the café where I read them passes a row of larch trees. It's not the shortest route, but it's the only one with a row of larch trees, and that is why I choose it more often than not. The tenth larch is the showstopper, the tallest, the most widespread, the most profuse in its leaf-making. I have known the trees for many years now, but it took the act of researching and writing this book to make me realise just how richly endowed a treasure store was right there on my doorstep. It was November before they started to turn, and it was the middle of the month before the storms found a way through the steep and deeply wooded sheltering bank that spares them most of the onslaughts of winds from south-west to north. By then, autumn had slipped across that watershed that divides its Indian summer from winter-waiting-in-the-wings. Since the first few days when snow had begun to camp on the mountains again, the air on the path by the larches had cooled noticeably, and the big larch had shed at least half of its needles. The effect was to reveal its true elegance, the more elegant because it was dressed in the softer-shaded seduction of a garment that now revealed more than it concealed. The legacy of all late-autumn storms is that softening of all their shades, cool fires wrought from the shades of flame.

The effect is nowhere more painterly than among larches. I had noticed it first a few days before when I had driven out to Loch Lubnaig under the first of the mountains to look at the snow, and found the loch – the epicentre of my writing territory, as I fancy it – in a particularly beguiling mood. It was flat calm, reflecting dark rock, dark bottle-green spruces, newly whitened mountains (but not their cloud-draped summits), and in the midst of all that the startling slashes and curves and twisted ropes of larches past their brightest autumn prime but still smouldering with embers of that shade of fire. Walking the forest road under the mountains, the surface would change colour every time it passed beneath a belt of larches, and their faded orange carpet had been badger-striped by the passage of forest vehicles, so that there were three orange stripes and two black. Now you know where Bassett got the idea for Liquorice Allsorts.

There was a small echo of that effect down the path by the ten larches, for the sparse foot traffic had made a dark stripe down the centre, between two wider swathes of that same faded orange shade. By the 20th of November, the big larch was the only tree that still held needles and they were now the colour of straw. I had the slightly out-of-leftfield notion of a beautiful woman with grey hair, and how, in the right circumstances, that can add elegance and dignity to the beauty.

That day, the siskins arrived in the larches. They came in a cloud, and their voices sounded like rain in the trees.

Larch trees have ripe seeds in autumn, a characteristic they share with Sitka spruce, and the spread of commercial plantation forestry across Scotland has boosted the Scottish population of siskins from around half a million to somewhere near five million in the winter when the natives are joined by swarms from mainland Europe.

I stood under the big larch watching these most engaging of small birds for so long that I started to shiver, and I dragged my thoughts away from the birds towards coffee.

◉ ◉ ◉

The second last day of November, the second last day of Meteorological Autumn, I walked up through high woods to photograph the mountains as the snow thickened and crept down to the mountains' waists. The summits of Ben Vorlich and Stuc a' Chroin kept emerging from cloud then slowly dematerialising again through softening focus as new piles of snow-cloud drifted across from the northwest. Then the process reversed itself painstakingly slowly, like the autofocus on my camera lens when it struggles to find a focal point. The foreground foothills were brightly sunlit, and sometimes the sun would creep up onto the snow slopes, tantalise for a few seconds then creep back down again. A big herd of red deer had gathered under Stuc a' Chroin, just below the snowline. I could read their minds: browse up here while the going is good. I had heard the weather forecast – more snow and temperatures falling tonight to "as low as minus twelve in sheltered Highland glens", and I thought, "Sheltered Highland glens like this one…" Of course, the deer knew all that already, and I suspected they would be down among the trees just above the little frontier town of Callander long before morning.

On the slow drive back over skittishly slushy roads down to the Carse, I had already decided to divert out among the small roads through the fields to where I had been watching one more gradual build-up of whooper swans over several days. When I got to the field in question there was not a swan in sight. It happens. I turned for home, rounded a sharp bend and was momentarily dazzled by a sudden burst of sunlight on a small pool of floodwater. As I drove past, I realised there was movement in the midst of the dazzling water. I found a spot on the grass verge where I could open the car door and look back. There were two swans there. I acknowledged my satisfaction at that little last-day-of-autumn glimpse, and was about to drive off when instinct stayed my hand and suggested a closer look. I could get to within about thirty yards of them without being seen, and a tree there would afford some cover while I took that closer look. They were Bewick's swans, the little goose-sized swans from Siberia. They are very rare fly-by-night visitors to the Carse, and more autumns and winters than not, there are none here at all. But my autumn pilgrimage had just bowed out with a pair of Bewick's swans. The pilgrimage was effectively done, for the next day I had to go to Edinburgh, and I could think of no finale more fitting.

Epilogue

Edinburgh:
Summertime in November

IT WAS THE LAST DAY OF NOVEMBER and he played *Summertime* on the trumpet. They told me it had rained hard for a week and the river was high. Edinburgh is apt to do that in November. No sooner is its long tourist season done than it doles out a loyalty test for the natives. Then, by way of reward, a day dawns like this one, the rain stops, the weary and wearying south-westerly holds its breath, trees straighten after a week of stooping and wading in mist. Up-tempo, the Water of Leith slaloms down from the Pentland Hills to the sea, booming and rasping through the city's canyons of built stone with their impossible bridges, pounding over its own weirs, surfing over its own rocks, plucking chairs from patios, footballs from gardens, saplings from banks; and a million leaves in every deep-fired shade of autumn are rafted seaward.

Herons stand on branches watching flotsam, waiting with the stalwart patience of their tribe for the river to relent, for shallows to resume. Kingfishers tremble on their accustomed perches in fear of drowning. Dippers, underwater foragers of distinction, are temporarily defeated.

You may find any or all of these briefly crowding in on the swans and lesser fowl of the tranquil pond at the Botanic Gardens. They all carry accurate street maps of the city in their heads. And they are all neighbours and passing acquaintances of the trumpet player.

He played by an open window on the ground floor in Hawthorn Bank Lane, which is quiet and steep and closed off and traffic-free apart from the river traffic – the birds and the varying thrusts of the current – and the cool trumpet on a still afternoon, when gently robust notes harmonised with the riversong as agreeably as honeysuckle blossom and summer rain.

I saw him for the first and last time that November day, when the rain forgot to fall and the wind to blow. His window, as I have said, was wide open, and reached down almost to the floor. Naturally, I looked in as I passed, but without stopping, which would have been rude. I walked on a few yards *then* stopped and turned and looked back. I saw him from behind and over his left shoulder, but beyond him on the far wall a mirror framed his face and his eyes were closed.

I had walked the riverside pathway from Stockbridge towards Dean Village, and it was there, crossing the cobbled street by the Dean Bridge, that the first notes of the trumpet glanced among the river's hoarse choruses, the way seams of light from a full moon leak through the thickest midnight clouds; between the overwhelming river and the stone walls that towered above its banks and threw its voice back at itself, the sound of the horn spun in and out of my reach.

A steep, narrow, cobbled lane high above the river ends abruptly in a steep stone ramp with a built cliff of flats on one side and an open, terraced drop to the river on the other. It was there, down by the foot of the ramp, and almost at water level, that the window stood open, a second bell through which the trumpet sound issued as burnished smoke.

So I turned my head as I passed without stopping, walked on a few yards, stopped and turned. He sat alone in a small room a few feet from the window, almost as if he was inviting the gaze of passers-by. He was good. He played with a pure, rounded tone, the notes well spaced, room for silences between phrases, jazzy embellishments here and there, but mostly loyal to the melody.

I decided he was American. He had been the leader of a trumpet section in a big band, perhaps, rather than a true jazz soloist. He had some kind of keyboard beside him, one that had been programmed to play a backing track – a rhythm section and some muted horns. There was a chart open on the keyboard in front of him, but his eyes were closed.

He looked about seventy, his crew-cut hair silvered and thinned, his stomach thickened by too many years of too much Jack Daniels on the rocks, his back straight, his trousers well cut, dark green cords, his shirt loose, silken, grey, button-down collar. He was oblivious to the day outside and its few passers-by, uninterrupted by my lingering pause beyond his window. He played on while his phantom orchestra kept time. Inside it was *Summertime*, outside it was *Autumn Leaves*.

He began a third chorus, building, but building softly, and where I wanted it to rouse and gather and reach further, it held back, lengthened and softened its notes and silences and drifted to a close, as gently as falling oak leaves, and there the river took them both. It took the music as it took the pale sun, broke it into fragments and cast it across the city, and northwards to where the firth casts off for the sunrise, the North Sea and the coast of Denmark.

His eyes opened then, and in the mirror they caught and briefly held mine. He lifted the trumpet an inch or two in acknowledgement. I nodded, mouthed a silent "thank you", turned, walked on up the autumn river and in my head it was summertime and the living was easy.

Acknowledgements

NO WORK OF LITERATURE speaks to me more tellingly of the landscape in which I grew up than Violet Jacob's poem *The Wild Geese*, which was first published in 1915 by John Murray in a collection called *Songs of Angus*. It is quoted here with reverence and gratitude.

Other Scottish writers whose work has enhanced my life one way or another, and enriched these pages, include:

GEORGE MACKAY BROWN, who is simply my favourite writer and the writer I read most;

GAVIN MAXWELL, my original inspiration when I read *Ring of Bright Water* as a teenager, and whose writing has revealed new truths and depth with the passing years (thanks to Eland Publishing Ltd and the estate of Gavin Maxwell for permission to quote from *A Reed Shaken by the Wind*);

SETON GORDON, who is surely the founding father of all modern Scottish nature writing;

FRANK FRASER DARLING, a pioneer of conservation thinking as well as a fine writer (thanks to Little Toller Books for permission to quote from *Island Years*);

HUGH MACDIARMID, arguably our best poet since Burns (thanks to Carcanet Press, copyright holders of his books).

And no Scot who has ever lifted pen to paper with literary intent these last 250 years is without debt to ROBERT

BURNS, the guardian angel who watches over all of us. Among those with whom I share a profound love of Burns was JOHN MUIR, revered today as a disciple of nature in two continents.

Furth of Scotland, I have quoted often from *Autobiography* by Margiad Evans from the English-Welsh border country, and do so again here in admiration of her exquisite touch and rare sensibility. And Hugh Johnson's *Trees* is simpy a masterwork.

I edge closer to poets and artists with the passage of time. W.B. Yeats and Thomas Gray crept into my thoughts as I wrote this book (I still think Gray's *Elegy Written in a Country Churchyard* is the best poem ever written in English, not that I've read them all, of course), as did Paul Cézanne and Ansel Adams. Adams's fellow countrymen Douglas Culross Peattie, Ralph Waldo Emerson and David O. Carroll are also gratefully acknowledged. Thanks too to the National Gallery of Art in Washington D.C. for the material accompanying its retrospective exhibition of Mark Rothko.

Friends whose enthusiastic support for this book provided the kind of sustenance I imagine all writers need include Jim Perrin, Holly Schaaf of Boston University, and Polly Pullar. Friends who are no longer with us but who also helped to shape my thoughts include George Garson and Pat Sandeman.

My working relationship with my publisher, Saraband, continues to prosper. Sara Hunt is the kind of publisher I have been looking for all my writing life. Saraband editor Craig Hillsley drew the short straw again but took my copious flaws in his stride, the obvious ones and the occasionally inexplicable ones. And my literary agent Jenny Brown's relentlessly positive perspective is a priceless asset for any writer to be able to rely on. Thanks to you all.

Finally, the presence of my father made an extraordinary impact on me while I was working on this book, and forty years after he died at that. Thanks, Dad. And lest you think mine was a one-parent family, my mother is everywhere in these pages, for she was the one who instilled in me a love of reading, music and art. I imagine few writers are so blessed.

JIM CRUMLEY has written more than thirty books, many of them on the wildlife and wild landscape of his native Scotland. He is a widely published journalist with regular columns in *The Courier* and *The Scots Magazine*, a poet, and occasional broadcaster on both radio and television.